A HORIZON FILLED WITH NEBELOUS CLOUDS

ROB VOGEL

Paperback: 978-1-966652-66-3
eBook: 978-1-966652-67-0
Library of Congress Control Number: 2025903438

Ordering Information:

Prime Seven Media
518 Landmann St.
Tomah City, WI 54660

Printed in the United States of America

A selection of poetry and verse written by Rob Vogel

"We should have no regrets about the past, and no remorse about the present, but and unwavering confidence in the future."

(Jean-Jaurés)

CONTENTS

Dreamy sleep..3

Isolation..4

Moon 5

A hot day 6

The sky in autumn..7

Twilight sun..8

Tides...9

Another dream 10

Thoughts of summer 11

Living but not alive 12

My loving summer 13

Autumn is among you 14

Winter is approaching 15

Disappearing sun...16

Autumn ashes..17

Adieu..18

The harvest moon..19

My path 20

The return of autumn 21

My dream within a dream...................................22

Sunlight...23

Tears..24

Spring...25

Flakes of snow...26

Hidden winter..27

The springtime 28

Time locked..29

Flowers..30

The harvester...31
Light of the sun 32
Notice 33
The sweetness of spring 34
Rain..35
My spirit 36
The hunt 37
The traveler 38
Storm..39
The design...40
My thoughts 41
Summer sun 42
River...43
A new season...44
Thwarding winter 45
Just me..46
Apple harvest...47
Halloween..48
The sunlight 49
The line 50
Sunrise..51
My circular path 52
Autumn leaf 53
Winter...54
End of october 55
Waiting for autumn 56
Dreamer..57
Sunrise..58
Sentiment..59
Love..60
Heaven..61
Windy road..62

Romance..63
Thunder 64
Friendship...65
Sunset..66
Friends...67
Winter..68
Friendship...69
Dreams of winter.....................................70
Thoughts of winter 71
Freedom 72
A flower 73
The grove 74
Woman 75
Love lost...76
Cats 77
Souvenirs..78
Forever...79
Autumn 80
Autumn color 81
Freedom 82
Wintery thoughts.....................................83
Morning..84
The evening 85
Sunrise...86
Dreams...87
Freeing my soul.......................................88
The rose..89
Patience 90
Souvenirs..91
Dreams 92
Meeting 93
Nightfall 94

Fury of winter 95

End of summer 96

Lost love 97

Confused seasons 98

Fog 99

Frost 100

Mystery 101

Eternity...102

Winter's time 103

Dawn 104

Night...105

Sword of time 106

Timeless 107

Leaf's...108

Little angel...109

Words 110

Sounds 111

Winter sun 112

Twilight 113

Time of year (sonnet)...114

The traveller 115

Differences 116

My queen...117

Beauty 118

Amour 119

Fear 120

Time 121

Children...122

Dream times (sonnet) 123

Words (sonnet)...124

Promises (sonnet) 125

Walks 126

Souvenirs...127

Morning (sonnet) 129

End of summer (sonnet)................................130

Night dreams 131

Arrival 132

Romances 133

Men 134

End of autumn...135

Meditation (sonnet)......................................136

Storm (sonnet) 137

Winter (sonnet) 138

Autumn's fight...139

Her protest..140

Winter's day 141

Receiving nothing 142

End of summer 143

Love that summer (sonnet) 144

France (sonnet) 145

Beautiful..146

Lost love 147

Setting sun (sonnet) 148

Wine..149

Summer time past.......................................150

Stone wall...151

Thoughts...152

December day...153

Last bit of summer 154

Hope 155

Friendship...156

Sweet music...157

Pain 158

Sunset 159

A melancholic year...............................160

Magic 161

Demons 162

Desire 163

Time 164

Autumn fades 165

Charm..166

Autumn's finished 167

Snow...168

Trembling heart..................................169

Night...170

Nightfall 171

Sunset 172

Dark nights......................................173

Unable 174

Autumn's dreams 175

Dewdrops 176

Moonlight..177

Hidden...178

White woman 179

Moonlight..180

Living 181

Forest secrets 182

The sky in autumn................................183

Twilight sun......................................184

Tides...185

Another dream 186

Thoughts of summer 187

A HORIZON FILLED WITH NEBELOUS CLOUDS

A series of poems, sonnets and musings by Rob Vogel, created in English but based on the French and Italian mediaeval poetry style.

This collection of poetry and trifles, uses the palette, extraordinary range, and ambiguity of the English language.
These are written, while the author lives in the South of France,
where he also creates his drawings, paintings, and other literary musings,
many of them still unknown.

During that time, he has developed his own poetic style and is always searching for new ways of using words and expressions to convey his creative feelings and memories of his former life in Holland, Ireland, America and the UK.
Often lost in his own imagination,
or as one of his beloved French poet once said:
"Venez, chère grande âme, on vous appelle, on vous attend"
(Come, great and dear soul, we are calling you, and are waiting for you).
With ventures into unknow ideas and experiences to excite the audience,
with new ideas, dreams and his past life.
The poetry attitude of Rob Vogel is often free but not always happy.

Often called confused, patchy and rigid, but as living in the south of France,
amidst the vineyards, forests and mountains can be a confusing experience;
After his life changing affairs, he became facinated by the elasticy of poetry and wanted,
to describe the pleasures of poetry and the direct discripton of life general.
Poetry often becomes full of a questions, full of form althought many people think of form as beauty
visualy created and shaped.
But beauty in poetry more the structure and shape of the written work.
Vogel's interest in french poetry is related, to the past poetry of the 1800 that was creative but not really read and rarely published in larger amounts and was often unsold,

Nowadays in the modern language, trying to use modern words is complex, often imprecise of feeling and emotions and we have to fight to explain the business, that is oft full of gaps and shadows, and we writers only vaguely know the complete sentence we want to create.
We often dream of the coldnes we feel but we know what we see is the beauty of what we write!

A lyrical work shows a whole range of words, rhythm's and associations, that only exist in that particular language, producing word interplay and spaces for meanings not expected.

Vogel's work has oft that half-finished halo of mystery and pearly gloom. Join me in this course
of his conjectures of poetry in this first of the bundles is called *"A horizon filled with nebelous clouds."*

DREAMY SLEEP

Let us gently feel that love so deep,
trees will branch over of what we'll keep;
shadows deepen as the night fall,
while we hear nightingale's soft call;

Gentle wind waft, grass sways and dew clings,
but most mortals only feel night's chilly sting;
soon the sun will wake and kiss that golden dawn,
then wings 'll rise and meadow's spawn;

Now our dreams are over, and sun 'll hide unbidden,
after that froth of love, unbeknown of what's hidden;
let us dance and laugh in morn's golden light,
around that aspen and wheedling flute on that day,
so bright;

I breath in that wind that's twisting your hair,
of the woman I seek during that night so fair,
my sight fails, in that dreamy light,
as you smile at me, softly kissing, with eyes dark and
bright.

ISOLATION

Isolation, I am lost in a nostalgic
haze that surrounds me,
confined by it, I do not hear, a pool
of thoughts separates my soul;

The fingers of the dazzling
summer's heat, seek me out,
encompassing me, probing and burning;

I am sinking and drown immersed
in my own thoughts,
dreaming of silence and the secret
pleasures hidden for now.

MOON

The full moon spread full and bright,
and the solemnity of the night is like a river;

Flowing through a silent town,
where cats secretly hide during the night;

As they follow those devious hidden furrows,
an illusion perhaps, I am immersed into myself;

Within my thoughts I do not hear,
anxious and silent for ideas that are to come;

The radiant night's stars reflected on the mirror like river,
illuminate my coat of darkness;

I fall back to sleep, and dream.

A HOT DAY

The day sears like boiling liquid,
and simmers in the air where it lingers;

The land oscillates and crunches,
the sunlight, like searing water, cascades down;

Streams of light, sizzle and absorb me,
burned and crumpled leaves flutter down in that still air;

Hiding the azure sky streaked with white lines,
I rush forward, to absorb that pleasure of life;

Yellow, golden, and white,
grasping those radiant sun beams of pleasure.

THE SKY IN AUTUMN

In that chilly Autumn's sky, devoid of sound,
countless stars shine cold and round;

With your hand in mine, we saunter,
aimlessly meandering, looking for the star that shines
louder;

These days will not bring Spring,
but we will endure the harsh days that Winter will bring;

Angels will sing when you are near,
together we do not fear.

TWILIGHT SUN

Like the disappearing twilight's sun,
and those glistening impenetrable stars of the night;

Your words touch me like a cool mountain spring,
as an Autumn day, filled with tender rain;

I wait for the emerging flower,
drowned by that rain;

Before Summer's blossoms approach,
flowing out to eternity.

TIDES

Tide rising slowly, engulfing my sanctuary,
fear fills my being,
all is outside, I am protected by my bastion,
stones impregnable by nameless forces;

The tide, my treacherous consort,
reluctant to follow my paths,
Lurking at every corner,
lessening my island of hope;

Swallowing my castle,
engulfed by the never-ending sea.

ANOTHER DREAM

Wind rushes through my life, like a dance of happiness,
cherishing every precious second;

But the bleak winter days are full of fear and wary
dreams,
my bastion 's broken and torn asunder on that fateful
day;

Tide rushes in engulfing and drowning my trusted
fortress,
wind surges through my life invigorating but
distrustful, I would say;

Rebuilding this stony rock,
a task completed within my dreams.

THOUGHTS OF SUMMER

Summer when will I see you again?
alas, my dreams move along paths uncharted;

Trampling those precious blades of summer's grass,
autumn, the austere one, will block my tracks;

Gone are my dreams of briny air scouring my
uncovered head,
will I see you again, my dear Summer;

And feel your bright rays searing my skin,
I am safe inside my dreams;

I Dream of that Summer.

LIVING BUT NOT ALIVE

My soul harbors a hidden secret,
nurtured over time and like surf rising slowly up from
the expanse of rumpled water;

Crushing my conscience overwhelming and austere,
I am bearing this exquisite secret like a shadow
engulfed by my dreams;

Asleep but no longer there,
my heart is filled with hope and courage, but not
daring to seek;

I pass time weak and weary, hence I will not ask nor
expect,
as she will read these lines but not understand them;

The salty air ruffles her hair, and create patterns in
the luminous summer's sand,
tormenting my soul, living but not alive.

MY LOVING SUMMER

Tears gush out of my eyes in a never-ending tide of
saline water,
I embrace summer's light, my dearest one;

Warm luminous beams play on the golden beach,
I wish not to see them perish, as the wintertime advances;

Slowly and insidious hiding its path and chilly intentions,
I want to embrace those playful rays of Summer;

And the rich chords that will praise the passing of
each month,
chords that will expire with each hour succumbed to
the frigid intention of Winter;

Like passionately love extinguished and cold,
winter, my hands are too weak to hold it back;

Coldness engulfs me,
my voice broken and crushed;

When will you return, my dearest Summer?

AUTUMN IS AMONG YOU

When that hourglass beat away the time,
hiding those hideous hours of the night;

Behold, the dreadful night's secret beauty is revealed,
when lofty trees sway in Autumn's wind;

The summer's beauty is girded with pain,
her beauty questioned by me;

Will the sweet winds of the autumn cut like a knife?
cutting down the summer's beauty, I ask;

Among the ruins of summer,
discover the change of time;

Autumn is among you,
will it slow down Winter's advance?

WINTER IS APPROACHING

Upon the restless swell of the sea,
I am seeking my expanse of tranquility;

Slowly drifting for an eternal time,
veiled, to hide my hopes;

In the morn the shining knights go to prowl on that
perpetual twisting path,
not finding me as I came by night, amidst starlight;

My veils are moved by that everlasting time,
you came to seek me on a dreamy bow of green leaves;

Heralding your intention of Autumn, the wretched one,
how do I find love in all this bleakness, I wonder;

Tranquility escapes and the mad sea proclaims its fury,
ripping away my trusty walls;

Terror fills my heart!

DISAPPEARING SUN

Like the disappearing Summer's sun,
and the glistening impenetrable
lonely stars of the warm night,
your words touch me like a cool mountain spring,
an Autumn's day filled with tender rain,
I wait for the emerging flower,
drowned, before summer blossom approach,
following out to eternity.

AUTUMN ASHES

In the Autumnal ashes,
against the sanguine swirls of the dying light;

I see the bleak silhouettes to the oaks,
sinister bleeding scars in the late sun's glow;

Branches twisted in semblances of agony,
gone are the dreams of an idyllic world;

That once was in my vision and now it fails me,
hidden are the treasures I still seek;

Do I see love deep within their slumbering minds?
in the height of the sky;

Hawks glide on their eternal paths,
leaves 're withered and bereft of life.

ADIEU

In the hours of the Autumn when nature dies,
with its slow and creeping departure,
my dreamy veils cover's her colorful allure,
I see the dying bowls of departing sunlight,
a friend's farewell;

I mourn the long span of sorrow, till she rises again,
I look back with envious eyes to the Summer's days
that once were,
I mourn the days with dying hope,
the days of promise will rise again while the insidious
Winter lurks,
hidden in its secret cloak surreptitious and unfair;

Alas, soon the mighty light will rise again banishing
the glacial power of the nights,
my veiled dreams tell me of her beauty and pleasure,
in the burning light of my lost friends,
once more my thoughts return to those Summer nights,
farewell my Summer, my friend.

THE HARVEST MOON

The harvest moon is rising in its first quarter stubborn not to rise fully soon,
autumn air is piercing the wood's darkness with its flow;

Yes, the days wane and the pale sun's feeble light fades, as Summer dies,
her last veiled days find allure without finesse;

A farewell with sorrow,
she will arise again, and we will drink out of her chalice of golden nectar;

Flowers fall like harvested corn full of hidden promise,
can my soul understand and absorb the honey mild;

The angels watching me with unsheathed swords,
and the air so pure with the dying rays of Moon's beauty.

MY PATH

The full moon hidden behind a dank palisade of cedar
trees,
slowly riding higher, she reveals her dazzling beauty;

The cooling night embraces moons loving light
through the fragrant cedar sprays,
her rays fill the chariots of beauty slowly rising up,
on their way;

My shadowy form, hidden from her light moves like
a vague ghost,
a vibrant shape dreaming, revealing only what is needed;

Let me find a way,
when the prowling wind find my path;

Cracking boulders and uprooting trees destroying my
pathways home,
perplexed and confused I am;

The moonlight passes through me,
dressing my troubled soul;

Filling that chalice of sweet nectar for me to sip,
giving me warmth in the cool night, to find my way
home.

THE RETURN OF AUTUMN

Thunder's rumbling her sinister hidden drumroll,
nature's moaning Autumn's return,
yellowing foliage and sparse grass, dark days and
agile veiled clouds;
Days of somber tones,
I mourn the last gorgeous day of nature's farewell;

Sadness under the waning sun and its soft feeble light,
nature dies and waits for that subtle arrival of Winter's
time;
A farewell and a sad greeting to the deceitful frosty
tones of Winter,
there is no beauty on the lips of those chilly tones;

Those days I find no beauty or allure,
hidden is the soft green beauty of Summer's day, past;
I want to drink the last drop the Summer's cup of honey,
and look back with envious eyes,

Dreaming of air and sweet light that will return soon.

MY DREAM WITHIN A DREAM

Spring tide's surf tormented coast is waiting for the breach,
I stand amid her icy spray of briny water;

Holding within my hands the grains of golden summer sand that I cannot reach,
bringing the promise of warm pleasure later;

A dream, light and tender like an asp;
I stand amid the roar of the rising spate,

Holding those grains within my grasp,
has one of those pitiless waves found a gate?

Sealing spring tide's fate,
It is my dream within a dream.

SUNLIGHT

Time of sunbeams and luminous light has ended,
gone the rich glory and freshness of my dreams;

Beautiful and fair, like a mountain stream on a starry
night, it was,
I hear echoes of sweet times past;

Autumn the harvester, is among us,
skies reddened in fiery hues as if on fire;

Forests shedding their gaudy leaf's array's,
withered leaves cover the disenchanted meadows;

Time is in suspense, agitated with fear,
for hope and the lingering love past;

The iron door of the north is bare,
concealed light hiding like a melancholic dream;

Rain flows and rivulets dancing in their wayward round,
the night stars shall be dear;

My soul will be given to that cruel icy wind;
and will wither like a flower.

TEARS

I will not grieve but rather find strength in what remains,
in slumber does my spirit heal;

I look to mother earth as if she has no purpose,
my eyes cannot choose but to see the honeyed rays of
summer sun;

Where did you go my Summer?
I paid no heed and did not see her depart;

Autumn has arrived, the revealer,
perplexed I look at the changing sky;

Dark brooding and forbidden,
terror and victory are united without light to guide me;

My unchartered freedom falters in the sight of such
dread,
the breathless nature's dark abyss;

I sleep among the sunless hills,
beside the river that glideth at its own free will.

SPRING

Under the fickle spring's sunlight, I walk,
the gay light glitter through the young raindrops,
that did not fall in winter;

Gray bricks of the avenues shining wet and glistening,
I walk in the golden flecked sunlight,
dashing to avoid the rain,

Spring time is here,
the roiling clouds of sky still frowning,
where their master 's gone;

Cold wind is funneled through the narrow lanes,
of budding trees and newly found life,
I stand still and cold at the river;

Wondering will I dare.

FLAKES OF SNOW

Storm driven are the flakes,
  Carried in their billowing blanket,
    Is that love, the sightless one,

      Lost in the envelope of icy crystals,
        Transported in its white sheet of promise,
        Soft as a caress towards the hope of summer's sun,

    Reality flashes by in an instant,
  Flowing under the sun,
I have stopped dreaming.

HIDDEN WINTER

We sink into the darkness of Winter,
distressed, the bare trees creating bizarre shadowy
patterns,
having lost their withered leaves;

Goodbye, brightness and colours,
sunlight caught into the icy inferno, unable to see any
hope,
winter will now invade my soul destroying my
thoughts of peace;

Hate, chill and dark days are my future,
I shudder when my heart feels like ice,
But my spirit is like a tower, unyielding in the gale;

Tireless fighting the battering of winter,
but my hidden memories of beauty are now all bitter,
I see the fading rays of the golden sunshine;

Autumns last ecstatic rays of tenderness,
mysterious and obscure for me, like a farewell.

THE SPRINGTIME

Gleaming sunshine bright and clear,
the new and joyful season is here;

Silver drops on a golden network of scales,
it has come before it's time, out of the dark dales;

Birds will sing merrily hoping to dwell here,
full of fresh scents and budding trees there;

While the whispering air says, do not be daunted,
we do not snare, but still the raindrops fall uncounted;

Spring has arrived dappled with black,
dark clouds gather, with the complexity they normally
lack;

The wind is still waiting for the sign,
as Winter hides, beyond, in her own white shrine.

TIME LOCKED

Time's folded like a coat,
wrinkled, unkempt and remote;

The sun is shining its watery light about the corner,
trembling as if in prison with nothing to adorn her;

Locked up deprived of its own vision,
but cannot be lost, knowing the impending collision;

We cannot avoid the blackened traces of the old,
Those fires recent, that were once there, uncontrolled;

I regret the emptiness of the sunny roads,
without windowpanes to reflect my soul or past abode;

Now the rising tide has diminishing my home,
soon swallowing those stones, where I so oft roam;

I lean and listens to the emptiness,
of the sunken stony mirrors and seas slipperiness.

FLOWERS

Flowers their fleeting
existence brief and compelling,

Reeling in confusion I am,
watching their petals fall,

Stalks doomed and crumpling at my touch,
autumn is harvesting their beauty,

Warm sun and azures skies surround me,
but the tormenter has arrived erecting a churning sky,

Dark clouds arrived at their appointed time,
will my flower survive the glacial tempest?

Dandelion swaying looking up at the auspicious clouds,
but hope is not there,

Winter is descending on us, aloof, cruel and harsh.

THE HARVESTER

Robust like awesome giants, my trees stand,
strong against the fierce blast in this saline land;

The trunks of these mighty plants,
laugh at the fierce tempest, never pliant;

The branches sway in the tumultuous gale,
singing their tune softly in the dale;

Autumn the harvester has arrived,
changing the tune every year I have lived;

The season is calling me by name,
for those that listen to her tale, it will not be tame;

Nature can't be restrained.

LIGHT OF THE SUN

At this early hour, the sun's golden beams dance in
the frosty air,
far away thought the Autumn's mist I can see her lair;

While the gardens full of withered leaves meet their
last date,
we slowly see their umber colour fade;

Leaves of copper and blood red, alas, now dead as if bled,
rain is dousing me no matter where I go or where I get;

Fair light sparkles down from natures rosy sky,
lighting the bare branches from which the last
swallows will fly;

The rays of sunlight in austere lines,
die severed and neat, cut off as if they were a fork's tines.

NOTICE

Up near the sky we hear the morning sing,
the tolling of the bells, I sit and wait for what it will bring;

Watching the veiled mist drifting into my heart,
while a river of dark smoke floats upwards hiding its part;

Boats with long masts straight and tall,
riding the swell waiting behind the wall;

Windows and stars disappearing one by one,
tidal streams are approaching the shore looking for
their beds, but finding none;

Seasons pass slowly until Winter enters with its frigid
gusts,
I hide by candlelight waiting for it to finish its rush;

Dreaming of the darting birds and the blossoms still,
orchards with swarms of bees, now it's just a memory
to fill.

THE SWEETNESS OF SPRING

May the sweetness of spring be the charm of my days,
I remember the caresses of the early sun stroking my skin;

How the glowing embers,
of the dying sun, warm my heart;

Those evenings of pink light softening my soul,
I feel the evoked blissful moments of peace;

Now hidden behind a stone wall,
will I be born again to this endless sea of sweetness;

And will I remember drinking from the golden cup of
luminous nectar?
or will I follow the twisty path of pain;

Encapsulated in the frozen word of snow,
I dream of sweetness.

RAIN

Rain, deep, hidden and secret cut my soul in two,
my forest where the trees are bend in half;

Silently walking in the moon's glow,
I sigh forlorn when light reveals;

Thunder peals in the distance not revealed,
behold a rainbow in the sky;

A skylark warbling up high,
giving hope, never to forget;

So was it when I got there first,
and so is it when I grow older;

The sky rejoices in the mornings birth,
my sun rising calm and strong;

Golden sunlight easing my pain,
yet, I persevere and find what I want.

MY SPIRIT

The slumber sealing my spirit,
once I could meet him there,
but he has dwindled and decayed;

But I persevere and find what I may,
wandering about alone and silently,
I rise up and drag both earth and bough;

To build my shady nook,
creating my own worlds, not realized,
out of those shadowy recollections, I question;

With the splendor of the young grass,
dark clouds gather on the horizon,
I will still have my lonely thoughts within these barren
hills.

THE HUNT

Within my shadowy vale I once stood,
facing the tempest that's arrived through that northern
iron door,
winds blow, water roils, clouds are hiding their thoughts;

Yet they are nothing,
these evil powers will subside within my mind,
the omnipresent murmur of nature will not dwell there;

I see the bright light of stars,
and the glory and the freshness of my dreams,
within it all, meadows, groves and streams rejoice;

Things I have seen but see no more,
wandering lonely like a cloud floating high above the
sod,
along the margin of the bay;

I hunt, startle and way-lay the unwary who lay.

THE TRAVELER

I travelled to a place far away,
moving quickly from lay to lay;

The air moves quickly, in most of the places,
but for me too slow, in most cases;

I ask, will I be there soon?
or should I be gone by balloon;

I should not have waited,
and ignored the trap that was baited;

But I'll be there, when the sun is asleep,
in that place over there, which they keep.

STORM

The sky plain and gray,
nature is keeping its breath, hiding its thunder, they say;

Heaven is floating, trouble is coming at its side,
when will it be the time to worry and hide;

Leaves are departing, descending from the trees,
covered the meadows enchanting like a golden fleece;

The thunder is hurried slow,
and is lighting is showing its golden glow;

Like a livid claw, light is striking those places only
the storm knows,
alive, as we know, natures burning water flows;

Rain is coming, rivulets of water finding their own way,
with nothing there to keep it at bay;

Dancing on the ground are drops enjoying their fall,
when will it end, I asked, but it was not my call.

THE DESIGN

Summer sun dazzling and bright, a sight to behold,
melancholy creeping into my mind, so I'm told;

Flowers evaporate like flowing violin sound,
I shudder at these thoughts, all around;

The sky so lovely, sad and tender,
I hate the vast, dark voids of the drawings I render;

Imagination my eternal companion deviant,
hiding its nature from me, odd but gallant;

Deceitfull dark clouds slide among my vision,
filled with promise but hiding their decision;

Time is here shaking on its stem,
events shrouded, arduous to remember them;

I live among frequent talks of things that never die,
and a world that does not cry.

MY THOUGHTS

Rain, soft, gentle but persistent,
unlike the sun, I cannot stop or resist it;

When will it end, I am wondering,
will the golden sunshine reappear, I am pondering;

Tracing patterns on my windowpane,
never ending streams of hope that I try to erase in vain;

During those days that are cold and dreary,
I am looking at the people outside who are wet and weary;

Pining for those golden days' past,
doing things that did not last;

In all love rain must fall,
but we remember all those things no matter how small;

My thoughts clinging to the past,
knowing it would not last.

SUMMER SUN

Summer sun where have you gone,
you pedantic fool, predictable, but not always there;

Your golden dazzling light is eclipsed by the dark
Autumn clouds,
my eyes are blinded by your beauty;

Will, I see you again, I wonder?
perhaps you have gone yonder;

Watching the Winter clinging at your skirts,
your beams so reverend and strong are slipping away
from me;

Winter is ready to strike, while I look across the
endless barren fields,
cold winds heralding the time is here, Winter, the
bitter and cruel one, has appeared;

It was hiding behinds its crenelated cold dry-stone
walls of the north,
will, I see you again my cherished Summer?

RIVER

I watch the dark calm waves of the sea flowing and
going forth,
while I hide under the veiled clouds approaching from
the north;

Clouds approach like a dark rushing river,
hiding their intentions from me forever;

Floating in that shadowy brook I watch fledglings
beating their wings in vain,
I am holding that thin ray of hope, that is impossible
to regain;

The golden stars and the secret songs will always be
there,
to find and behold the beauty, so rare;

I will move further, without progressing
in the directions that are difficult to know without
guessing;

The last of the sails still floats in the air,
alone, free to take the wind, if they dare;

Among the birds and the salty wind,
we are blind, never knowing what we will find.

A NEW SEASON

In the richness of life, seasons change, with a blizzard
of ripe fruits,
when the varied hues of the forest leaf's, Autumn
passes us by;

I watch the paths carved by the hawks who follow
their ethereal tracks,
while surrounded by the crumpled leaves, detached
and lonely I wait,

On those trampled and harvested land, barren and
destitute, time stops,
the stags sound, preparing for their futile duels;

I weep while Autumn passes, land culled and trampled;
winter, like a frozen train rolls in our life,

Boisterous and unstoppable, gathering his frigid mates;
dark clouds like obscene spirits spreading their
tentacles around,

The iron door has been opened ending my lonely wait;
a liquid golden moon moves gently among the bare trees,

Creating hideous shadows, hiding Winter's cold intentions,
a new season has arrived.

THWARDING WINTER

It's a desperate attempt of the Summer to thwart Winter,
the Summer's changing of the seasons has failed;
The maker and his companions have arrived,
bare trees and dark fog surrounding me, a world veiled;

Winters with his icy touch is descending,
turning my world into a shapeless blanked of frigid
beauty;
My world is gone still,
while the cold earth sleeps below its blanked of snow;

The moon's dying light gleams dimly on her tangled hair,
as she hides in the barren fields;
Frost cracking open the soil looking for life that is
not there,
tree roots exposed beside the frozen track silent and black;

The sun's feeble attempts are sinking behind the grim
clouds,
nights are shedding their warmth;
While I wait in the bitter winds and under the naked sky,
for my beloved Spring to return.

JUST ME

Along the wet and lifeless shore,
I dance following that windblown ruffled sand, I adore,

While the winds of Winter roar,
I feel safe on that beloved but barren land, we all look for;

While the raindrops fall in ever greater speed,
my hair covered with water, I have to concede,

For a fool there no need,
to go to the world of watery drops, we all agree;

Love is lost as soon as it is won,
the warrior dies before the battle is done,

While pleasure and fun are all but gone,
and we realize the deception of all these things bygone;

But I do not care as I have not known this Wintery place,
and crowds that gathered, once she showed here face;

As I will not be there I will be gone,
walking to my vista in a land I called Aragon.

APPLE HARVEST

Apple trees heading towards the sky,
and disappearing into the distance, I spy;

While I cannot forget that strange sight,
with morning frost is showing like a blight;

On my way, I went to that distant lay,
hoping nobody would tell or say;

Picking in the harvest great,
apples russet and ripening late;

All around me left and right, apples are round and bright,
cherishing the feel, lifting them down, trying to do it right;

Apples appear and disappear as they fall,
while I roll in that grass far too tall.

HALLOWEEN

Autumn, the harvester, has come,
while I was asleep and waited, the Summer has gone;

Trees die and spill their golden goods,
as souls emerge out of the woods;

To feast at the sugary snacks,
until sunrise they can fill their never-ending sacks;

While wood smoke drift slowly like the ghosts,
that appear like shadowy images on a walls and posts;

In the thinning air during darkness frost kisses the wilting weeds,
like a cold-hearted lover taking only what he needs;

They creep out of their hallowed liar,
those ones that should not be there;

Sunrise is approaching, golden beams flowing over the barren fields,
it is time to return and hide in darkness behind their shield.

THE SUNLIGHT

On the last of the summer's eves,
we walk among those golden leafy paths;

I am dreaming of the azure skies, I miss so much,
the tang of salty air that can carry me upwards, and
fills my bare soul;

Waiting for that moment the sun will disappear,
enduring the pain and sorrow, I am;

Among the cooling nights filled with my torment,
my happiness flees like a ghost;

Unwanted and unseen,
returning to its hidden haunt;

I wilt and thrive all at once,
no knowing if my joy will be certain;

But as long as my mind can embrace the sunlight,
my thoughts will be as one.

THE LINE

We are as one,
a line that meanders in the middle;

Steps sounding in the night,
an open-door shiver;

A body moves,
the sun, our golden protector is holding us tight;

Those bright sparkling rays of light,
giving color wherever they fall;

Will her fire be extinguished?
or will the shadow slips away;

Bright rays of a force unknown,
a fragile power without strength;

As I breath icy air surrounds me,
like a wall of frozen glass;

We are no longer as one,
I have broken my line.

SUNRISE

The morning frost touches the last of the wilted grass,
I walk, along that devious twisted path;
Passing dying trees with their gnarled branches still high,
I trudge on, eyes fixed at that horizon I glimpsed from
far away;

Waiting for the golden glow of the rising sun,
beams of translucent color will touch my body;
Like a painter's brush stroking every branch and leaf
I pass,
alone and unknown, I walk on, regretting that the day
will be like night for me;

The sun fills my soul with hope,
but will I discover an empty sea forsaken by the sun;
Boats floating on that water, unable to point home,
moving under the hideous dark clouds;

Waiting for the sun to rise,
full of hope and promise.

MY CIRCULAR PATH

I follow my curved path around,
the circular whirl of life;

Never seeing it all,
I follow the ships on that never-ending sea;
Ships without rudder or restraint,
to find my hidden haunt;

A whole world seen through my eyes,
directions vague and veiled;
Innocent instructions confused and muddled,
a hunter follows the source of prey;

Will the simplicity of life return to me?
like the morning dew on the newly born grass.

AUTUMN LEAF

Autumn, leaf's will fall, wither, and die,
nights lengthen, days shorten;

While the last sunshine warms the barren fields,
Leaf's move and frolic in their windy dance;

Falcons circling aimlessly on their pointless tasks,
moon rises slowly, hesitating in its path;

I listen to the song that only I can hear,
the iron door is opening calling in the northern wind;

The leaf's dance has ended,
in the frigid cold wind, I see;

That snowy blanket is arriving,
hiding my future beyond all reach.

WINTER

Red and golden leaves are dropping, covering the
barren fields,
sinking into Winter's darkness, they wilt;

Invaded by winter's frozen whims,
sun disappears in an icy inferno covering its golden coat;

My hearth will be frozen over,
a river stopped in time;

The sweet beauty of Summer has gone bitter now,
I shudder to accept the task;

My spirit is weak unable to face that facade of coldness,
I will miss that warm sunshine on a calm sea;

Falcons ride their lofty paths not knowing which way
to go,
winter has invaded my being, destroying my inner
thoughts;

Will, I feel the beauty of Winter's frosty gifts?
fading all color of my beloved world;

Flakes drifting down from those angry clouds,
hiding all I can see.

END OF OCTOBER

While I travel across the world, we do call home,
setting and trimming my sails, unsure of where I can roam;
I create my own private and secret places,
in the barren sea, I dwell, leaving nowhere any traces;

While the golden Autumn moon is rising, with her
toothless smile,
ghosts and witches are hiding from his pale and
pointless guile;
We live in this golden world and see the falling
Autumn leaves,
crumpled and dying is that surrounding multi-hued sheaf;

The jack-o'-lanterns grin during the night,
filling the darkness with their eerie flickering light;
Bare trees hiding are in the shadows trying to touch
the evening sky,
while we go to people who fear our tricks, and are
unwilling to look us in the eye;

    To collect our sweet rewards,
    and singing our uncertain tunes always on guard.

WAITING FOR AUTUMN

While I wait under the nightly sky,
dreaming of that calm dark waters, were stars are sleeping;

Waiting for that elusive thought, I should remember,
I wonder will the pale Autumn moon be there;

A soft wind ruffles the last of the Summer's flowers,
while I walked across that silver desert;

I feel that luminous sunbeam,
warming the last of the bare empty fields;

The fragrant wind blowing around my body,
touching memories past;

While stardust is sprinkling my thoughts around me,
magical and unknown;

I dream silently, hiding my sorrow,
while seasons change and nature steps in;

The silent willows weep;
and the last of the summer's grass dies, Autumn has
arrived.

DREAMER

When I met her hidden and fearful on spring's early green,
sunbeams hiding my passage on those fresh green fields;

The indigo sky was singing as I walked on,
even silence has a tongue to haunt me, while I go;

A riddle of nature that I cannot solve,
and hiding my soul so I cannot see;

This and my heart and all the fields and meadows wide,
I am smitten with that place that was once a stream;

Gone and hidden now, yes,
I am a dreamer, awake and asleep.

SUNRISE

The honey golden sun breaks through the summer clouds,
her beams kissing the dew-covered grassy grounds;
With the speed that only nature knows,
she rises in her full glory, that shows;

The creator of all life we meet,
I feel the coolness of the dew at my feet;
And the soft and golden glow of her beams where they stack,
my heart skips a beat in tune with the time we lack;

While I choose a place intended for you, that is right,
And I'll will dance with you at twilight;
Till moonlight sets you free,
but I know it was your dream, and I agree;

It will not reveal your face,
or shows the truth and your grace.

SENTIMENT

My heart holds unto a feeling,
that my mind cannot explain;

While the angry clouds gather for their Autumnal meet,
I meander through life;

Not knowing my destiny or meaning of it all,
using the freedom until now, unknown;

I embrace every morning as if it is mine,
will it tell me what you really feel;

Will it all be revealed in times to come,
heavy rain drops fall, sinking in the sodden soil;

Feeding the barren empty fields of life,
giving me hope and faith to heal and grow.

LOVE

I have met you in my dreams,
and waited for you many a night;

While the dawn is smiling and the dew covers it all,
I am uncertain of what it all means;

The flower buds flutter, jasmine flowers with her
white wings,
and soft music, murmured far and wide;

The messages we mortals write,
filled with the intoxication of daily delight;

They are just re-appearing visions,
of things that are not real;

With my eyes firmly closed,
to those dreams that are not real.

HEAVEN

A rainbow comes and goes,
colorful but fragile, airy and clear,
Visibly amid the sky's blues,
untouchable we say, as it appears;

Like a child, it plays with our senses,
climbing into the suffused sunny sky, it does,
Breaking down our visual defenses,
making us often smile and cry;

In this frail world of ours,
we mortals all will suffer,
But the gracious welcome the world in which we are
often hurled,
we will accept the proclaimed welcome of nature,
Smile and lift our head for that endless springtime.

WINDY ROAD

The winding road I took, through this old and forlorn
wood,
I travelled among leafy tree's, and across sodden
barren fields,
sleeping behind soggy boughs, ancient but still good,
looking in the undergrowth seeing what it would yield,
trampling the grass in those meadows so green;

I should have gone the other path, 't was perhaps more
fair,
as I walk on this muddy track, dark and black,
I have lost my way, and my woman so dear,
not feeling the imagination, I had once, and now lack,
I have to return to the old ways, that I did recognize;

I am dreaming when I dance during twilight,
till daylight sets me free,
your eyes are glowing even when they'r shut tight,
hoping to see you fully, but it is not to be,
will I wake up from that dream soon?

Perhaps on the long way, hence,
I will find the tru love I seek,
but will then my friends return, and fight in my defense?
to shore up my dreamlike bulwark, grown so weak,
perhaps I can keep this dream for another day;

I am telling this all with a sigh,
as the fair road I took, has no end,
I cannot turn around from this route, that I cannot defy,
travelling along this road unsure where I go and what
I ascent, scattering my words and
leading my soul awry.

ROMANCE

No more can I face those romantic sorrows,
remembering your sweet and uplifting eyes,
without clouds or weeping rain that follows;

To walk the grounds on that path trodden often,
where our ancestors look on us again,
a painful vista of my future which they cannot soften;

Paths where love is departing from vision,
If the thought of love desert us that way,
let's break off all sense and go, avoiding collision;

Let use our inspiration to set us free,
curb those feelings of pain and rage,
knowing the glorious morning gives us the faith we see;

The sun's golden orb slowly descends towards the
horizon,
the last warmth of the summer rays are caressing my
skin,
as summer is disappearing in the sea behind boat mizen;

A low rumbling in the distance herald the arrival of
autumn,
the sound of thunder invades this last summer's day,
while soft rain starts to wet my bare head,
I cry and say goodbye to my summer.

THUNDER

The Autumn light sinks into its nightly dwelling,
lowering its golden globe without telling,
amid the dark clouds, she hides her golden shine,
while I long for those rays that are not mine;

The first cooling wind like ice strokes my bare skin,
making me shiver and worry about what's to begin,
a soft rumble is rolling around the trees,
will the lights of thunder appear and shatter my peace?

Looking skyward darkness covers my sight,
black sinking clouds touching me like a blight,
the first raindrops run down my face,
like tears, wrapping me into that liquid embrace;

Do I deserve nature's wrath, I wonder?
submerged into the ferocity of its thunder
I hide behind my stony walls and wait in
nature's icy call.

FRIENDSHIP

Friendship precious and good to hold,
a flower blooming in the Spring,
sometimes it is not always as we are told,
planting flowers not knowing what they will bring;

Summer has made it strong,
and sprinkled it with soft dewy drops,
branches trimmed, when too long,
it stands like a beacon against the treetops;

Grounded by trust and beauty unsurpassed,
help and care gathered and amassed,
we care for life, we sometimes shared,
like dew it's daily renewed;

We find the beauty that is always rare,
and love so often wrongly viewed but fair.

SUNSET

Sunset, the golden globe going for her nightly sleep,
sinking into her soft cloudy horizon bed, a curve, so
steep,
disappearing and hiding below the soft horizon line,
to a space we do not know, and is not mine;

My love has left me, I wonder, to a place unknown,
will, I meet her again, my beauty who is now all alone,
dead is like living, but not here,
it is something bigger and is something that cannot
be hold dear;

In my dreams, I suffer,
thought have become a blur,
a new beginning, Spring is appearing in the air,
imagination so full and so clear;

Diseases unknown and strange are here,
the maker's skill we cannot range, but fear;

FRIENDS

After all this time of writing,
I create it without fighting,

My writing, not exactly sublime,
It's built without real help of mine,

I was surprised and thrilled,
at your answers, so skilled,

After writing sheet after sheet,
your touch is surprising, and hard to beat,

You know what is required,
it is not a skill I have yet acquired,

For me there is no control,
writing more comes from my soul,

I don't think you will ever fully understand,
that you make me feel as if I live in another land,

Without you I don't know where I'd be,
and the next letter is hard to foresee.

WINTER

Soon the cold shadows will arrive,
hiding the warm sunny afternoons, we so love,
logs gathered for us to survive,
chestnut ripening within their cocoons,
gathered and peeled for the goodness we will derive.

Winter is coming, with hate and its icy grip,
my soul imprisoned within its cold imagination,
I shiver and detest his icy whip,
my mind hides within the frigid creation.

The moon vast and serene,
spreading her light to touch the waves crest,
her light reach places that are never seen,
finding that unknown meadow so I can rest,
my last hope of release from Winter's icy chest.

FRIENDSHIP

Friendship precious and good to hold,
like a flower, blooming in the springtime,
sometimes it is not always so, as we are told,
planting flowers, with not knowing what they will bring.

In summer friendships, like mountains, will be strong,
and sprinkled with its soft dewy drops,
branches trimmed when too long,
while the wind pushes against leafy treetops.

Friendship, grounded by trust and beauty unsurpassed,
will my help and care gathered and then amassed,
I care for a life, we sometimes share,
like dewy droplets, daily renewed.

DREAMS OF WINTER

The rising tide fills my mind,
destroying the beautiful dreams already there,
will Winter search and find;

My coat, my cover,
my hope and goodness,
I sleep deeply, till the morning;

Dreaming across the world,
there is no bird or plant,
that can we such a handsome white coat;

A coat like icy gleaming droplets,
only one season it will allow,
stilling brooks and rivers at that time.

THOUGHTS OF WINTER

Like a flash on my inner eye,
in my spirit the world stands,
a world of twilight and beauty;

While I tread along the hard edge of snowdrifts,
soft and gentle they say,
but I feel the anger and harshness within;

Snow so fragile and tender,
like the beaded bubbles at the brim,
that disappear on my caress;

Unknown calmness exists, inside that fragile husk,
to bruise and freeze my spirit,
that makes me live in utter solitude;

Today in the distance I saw her,
like a glittering part of an icy glacier,
cold and aloof slipping into the sea;

To disappear in the vastness of the ocean,
absorbed in that saline world,
a world of cold beauty and wonder.

FREEDOM

I love what I behold,
calm night and days of glee,
days covered by dragon's wings spree;

Protected and hidden away,
what more need I desire in this way,
the lark hiding in the briars;

Let's loose its carol's in tones ever higher,
and silences descents as its wants,
nature beauty and freedom, it flaunts;

Autumn leaf's twinkle in the mellow breeze,
and thus, in my eyes, there gleams,
a shadow of peace, it seems.

A FLOWER

Many years it grew in sun and shower,
nature helping, while I would cower;
flowers so tender, hiding in the weeds,
giving me the beauty, I desire so much to meet;

The feeling of delight,
the rivulets of scent, dance while I flight,
beauty fading slowly into the night,
while blue sky condenses, stealing all the light;

Flower color like a rainbow, in that dark sky,
all I see is the glittering, I sigh;
an unwanted tale you bring to me,
as an invisible bird that will doubtless flee;

A tale of beauty never told,
unknown is that divine moment the story hold;
all I see is the bright glittering in that smokeless air,
flowers wilt and are invisible, no matter where I stare.

THE GROVE

I listened to many a soft note,
while I reclined upon that green grove, in solitude;
that sweet mood and pleasant thoughts,
bringing sad thoughts to my mind;

Birds hopping and playing all around,
what they think I do not know,
their motion is a trill of pleasure,
but my soul like a wilting flower;

Looking for sustenance to survive,
I catch the briny air of the past,
and I must think all I can do,
I have no reason to lament here anymore.

WOMAN

It is time for rapture,
I do not dare to tell;
a woman 's like Spring, in love of every day;

Fresh as an early rose, they say,
beneath that early full moon;
let her walk that curving un-trodden path;

The path never used or gained by me,
she will be mine, as I will make,
a midnight star, so dear;

In slumber did my spirit soar,
but terror will overawe me, my hands feeble in fright,
waiting for that single sign of love.

LOVE LOST

My heart holds a mystery,
conceived love, unnoticed,
walking beside her, in anguish,
I pass time and will not know it,
not willing or daring to ask,
of a woman, so sweet;

However, she will not understand,
she cannot recite my verses,
as she is filled with pain and torment,
while I live my crazed life,
and care for only that brief moment,
of love sweet and tender,
gone and forever spend.

CATS

Like an invisible ghost,
she roams around,
gazing in places, we cannot see;

Attacking walls and floors raving mad,
charging into that inky night for no reason at all,
her black pelt invisible in the black shadowy darkness;

Absorbed, here and disappearing,
hiding in many nooks, to and fro,
she looks up when called;

While I see myself,
in those gold colored amber of her eyeballs,
wondering who I am.

SOUVENIRS

When I woke up that day,
we would walk those grounds together,
in uncomplicated way, we say;

We laugh and pause,
touching those raindrops running like tears,
thinking of croissants wet and sodden to be;

Following that well-trodden path,
of the unknown future,
because there's everything, and nothing to be said;

While we are together and apart,
while trees are bending backwards,
hoping for love and those silent echo's;

But we wait for the flowers to bloom,
as there are things to have to choose among them,
of songs unknown to me and you;

I think about the blue dawn,
and the silks that embrace us,
soon we awake in that morning light that I cannot hear.

FOREVER

The sea, that endless cerulean sheet,
caressed by the fiery sun,
am I free, I wonder, or held by that satiny light;

Hot and burning it is, with no escape,
I whisper during the nights, for freedom,
to free my spirit of that fiery beauty;

I long to look at that infinite sheet of stars,
the universe has claimed me, to endure her will,
life flows slowly past that empty beach;

Wind sings her mournful song,
Tidal currents looking for their nightly bed,
kissing the golden sand to rest;

Will the sea be gone by tomorrow, I wonder,
freeing me from that inexorable torment,
giving me time to breath in, those fragrant memories
I lost.

AUTUMN

Those long eves filled with golden light of glowing
embers,
those radiant sunsets full of warm light,
autumn the beauty of those four seasons;

Giving her elegance to us,
alas, my heart longs for times that evoked those
blissful moments past,
summers sunshine and charm to enjoy;

Now the night encloses me in with her sealed embrace,
but my voice will rise to be heard again,
my mind will embrace past beauty;

I do not wish it all to die,
love is the hymn of the night,
it is what the waves whisper to that sandy shore abroad;

And what the wind says to the mountains,
while forcing sails to carry forward the signs,
alas, my eyes are dry and my hands feeble now;

It makes me realize I live and believe in love,
of the woman whose eyes shine with sudden candour,
while I ignore her, and feel her angst;

Will, I see the golden glow of that fall evening,
and the flowers that bloom in spring,
as the day passes by and I stay still.

AUTUMN COLOR

Autumn a colorful show,
I hear its mournful sighing,
like violin's long whispers;

My heart is sinking languorous, pale with sorrow,
dark hours pass me by,
full of those crumpled golden leaves;

Leaves once youthful and green,
now shriveled and colored umber,
going to and fro in their last play;

The hollow tone of the midnight chimes,
remind me of that new day coming soon,
with winds that lifts and play;

Those leaves were once green and ripe,
I am here, while they suffocate and die,
and I grief of their past life and glory

FREEDOM

We walked on that rocky shore, devoid of softness,
we revel in the boundless expanse of saline glory,
heaving with that hidden power;

Waves follow their instinctive paths,
following rules of their tidal masters,
a world enslaved and imprisoned by the shore;

Freedom is given to birds,
sea can feed them but cannot stop their flight,
the clamor of the water in her fruitless quest;

Whipped up by countless winds,
but unable to break her bonds,
I mourn that muted song of waves, no longer free.

WINTERY THOUGHTS

Winter's time, when soil becomes granite,
streams transformed into glossy white marble,
covered with that soft icy blanket of white;

I gather in the forest's its woods,
to warm my body and soul,
while the farmers plough for their golden goods;

Dark eves hide my somber thoughts,
tumbling clouds decent, filled me with unease,
I look at that golden forest, still untouched, while
winter plots;

Trees waiting for that mighty aerial flow, denuding
their dream,
stealing their annual harvest soon,
ships masts shiver in the storm from abeam;

Forcing me to heel and turn alee,
I am not that mysterious tree to whom the wind speaks,
harvesting the ripe fruits for which I yearn while birds
flee;

It's time to shelter from the wintery fondling and say
goodbye,
while I watch leaves floating in the air like irrational
birds,
unable to steer or see their future, without them
pondering why.

MORNING

What little do I see,
a traveler of unknown haunts,
I rest in humble lays unbeknown to me;

My spirit impels me,
to watch that misty morning sky,
that will become a pale virgin sheet;

Untouched and unblemished,
while the lark sings,
songs that I cannot measure;

The budding twigs spread their arms,
to catch the morning air,
I have no reason to lament.

THE EVENING

So pure is this air, so quiet is this wood,
I shudder of the thought that when the moon rises,
I will see heaven, bare and devoid of stars;

Our sleep will be forgotten while we fill our soul,
with fragments of dreams as odd shaped art,
those dreams tell me of my troubled past;

Taken away by the pilgrim of the sky,
while the nightingale in her darken wood,
composes her songs I hear still;

On this beautiful evening calm and free,
I watch breathless with adoration,
the broad sun sinks slowly, going to her rest;

The gentleness of nature's heaven,
as I look at the smokeless air,
contemplating man's unconquerable mind.

SUNRISE

I wake up while the smiling morning shines,
birds sing their amorous songs,
while trees in their green attire, wait in cheerful rows;

Trough misty barriers I see her sunny face,
rising above the forest edge,
while boats are anchored in rigid lines;

Their masts reflecting in that calm sea,
waiting for that daily clamor,
with the omnipresent murmur of the waves;

When I cast my eyes,
I see, and will abide my thoughts,
not knowing where to go;

I retreat into my rocky abode,
looking eastwards see her face sparkling and fresh,
as I wait behind that shadowy bank, for the sun to appear.

DREAMS

It is not the greying clouds or the soft rain,
and the misty vistas among the rolling hills,
or those rocky outcrops;

I seek that long golden beach,
glorious sand, covered in that soft cloudy moisture,
while I chase that hidden fleck of sunlight;

Sun within that cloudy sky kissing my skin,
I will find it before the beach ends,
love will guide me along that empty river of sand;

A river that separates my dreams from reality,
alas, hidden in those misty clouds,
are the perilous hazards I must face;

I dream of those lonely fields filled with wild flowers,
while I wander along those green grassy banks,
thinking of the golden vision I once had.

FREEING MY SOUL

Clouds raking mountain tops,
waves confined by the shore,
fueled by those gyrating winds never seen before;

Twice or thrice I passed you by,
not seeing your face,
I was that traveler, a mask, disappearing without trace;

Like a shadow upon that meadow green,
thus, I walk on, seeking those windy coasts,
shores protecting, my memories lost;

Thoughts of those rigid masts,
unbending and stark,
waiting for the billowing sails to embark;

Gazing out over the sea, kind but oft cruel,
with curving waves crashing into the rocks
unable to see their foamy dock;

An unceasing flow toward the sand,
waves, bubbling and gurgling, trying,
to break that shore and stop my soul from weeping.

THE ROSE

Looked at that steep bank of sand,
sterile and barren on either hand;

I spotted the young grow,
that lonely rose starting early, but slow;

That sleek and tender thing,
startled in the morn, not able to wait for spring;

Sun still low and weak to see, yes 't was,
giving her hope, the fair lass;

But on that divine day,
down that slope he slit, in that tumultuous way;

The dog, squat and furry,
her brown eyes not seeing, as she was in a hurry;

Trampling that new and young grow,
the creator's life's first vow;

Destroyed in the growing light of the day,
that rose, unknow died, in her growing fray.

PATIENCE

Dark days and deep nights,
I long for that brightness of the sun;
birds gone to sleep while I wait until twilight,
windswept waves that turn white when run;
the distant sound of thunder is bright;

I wait until morn has woken,
when vultures circle my soul;
hiding the last flutter'ng of pleasure I stole,
along the cliff's edge I wander unsure of my role,
while clouds conspire to cover their goal;

There's no ship in sight,
when dusk reappears from behind that rocks;
the moon that rises yonder like a blight,
waiting for that ship it's mocks;
patience, like white wings drawn on white.

SOUVENIRS

Those warm late summer eves,
while I walk along those paths filled with golden leaves,
wind moving around m' bare head;

Silence is all I can hear, not thinking where to go,
yet, that infinitive love will be linked to me,
to my soul empty now and mute;

Creation, is the goal I seek,
dreaming, I will see first my steps, in a life so austere,
untrained, waiting for that first touch, I am;

What does it matter, life or dead?
those streams of endless summertime are forever there
for me,
renouncing that bitter thought;

Creation is like a blossoming flower,
an endless spring, flowing into rushing rivers,
love it, I vow, keep loving, after having so loved.

DREAMS

Those ethereal azure skies, deep and clear,
I hear the skylark, that herald of the sky,
why do we accept it in this frail and broken world;

Ignoring the sound of that nightingale, singing in its
shady wood,
grave doubts ruled those sweet dreams of mine,
while I am asleep in that watery grove;

The night sky 's like a velvet glove covering my soul,
while my freeborn mind creates patterns unknown
before,
no sound is uttered in that open portal of mine;

A deep harmony pervades my mind,
while I glimpse at those distant visions I desire,
will they elude my grasp, I wonder;

I see that silent spectacle, and gleam,
that shadow of supreme peace,
as I sleep 'mid unfading hopes.

MEETING

I wandered within those floating clouds,
while we're far apart,
but you are never far from my heart;

We will meet sometime,
alway when, and never now,
all those wonderful things you say;

If it is your touch that I would feel,
I'd embrace you, knowing it is not real,
I feel you are near although you're not;

As long as we are on this path together,
there's nothing we can't do,
and on this delightful day;

I cannot choose but think,
you caught me off guard, took me by surprise,
but will wait for that day we'll be together.

NIGHTFALL

On that lovely autumn evening, the shortest day's year
event,
when the last umber coloured leaves have fallen,
I look at the azure sky changing into that golden colour;

Dominated by that immense ball of burnished solar fire,
slowly sinking into her nightly resting place,
while the final beams splinter out of that golden sky;

As the sharp horizon line battles with the hazy valley,
changing those faint archipelagos into golden enclaves
of darkness,
I dream while scales of golden mail cover me;

Protecting me of that last elemental sword thrusts of
sunlight;
while fragments of clouds turn into darkness,
when night slowly falls into its rightful place.

FURY OF WINTER

Those beautiful old paintings lovely created,
crafted by those ancient masters, now gone,
portraying their leafy evening avenues;

Whilst mist floats like reefs in that calm sea,
obscuring the slowly sinking golden globe of light,
and darkness arises up out of that saline pool;

The blurred horizon line of steep mountain sides,
shown by the last of that sublime evening light,
alas, that dying evening light will soon be gone;

Summer light fades to be replaced by dark winter's hue's,
darkness falls, replacing those beloved broken sunbeams,
beneath that dark starry winter sky that is surrounding
me;

Waiting for the approach of those billowing clouds,
piled upon each other,
storms rush in to take the vacated autumn dwelling,
surrounded by cloudy field of sorrow;

Will, I survive this tempest of fury,
my skin feels like living ice,
tingling with passion to resist winter's ire.

END OF SUMMER

I am greeting nature's last gorgeous day,
gone are those golden leaves, disappeared into
autumn's grey,
bare branches evoke pain and sorrow seen silhouetted
against that evening sky;

While the waning sun send her out last warning cry,
we mourn for those long days of hope gone by,
the light of summer, no more than a sad memory;

As I walk my lonely path dreaming of warm days,
I mull over past blessings, once enjoyed,
winters veiled looks have little allure to me;

Will I depart, as you wait while the grass whitens
during the night,
I will walk my path, with my eyes fixed onto my own
thoughts,
unseeing and without hearing a sound;

Saddened, that summer has ended,
whispering the confession that no one will hear,
during that icy night, full of human prayers past.

LOST LOVE

I am submerged into the cold of that frozen winter's
night,
we have said our last good-byes to the summer past,
coldness invades my body gently penetrating my inner
being;

Sunlight like a scaffolding surrounding me, but there
is no warmth,
my spirit protecting me in a rocky bastion,
my heart is frozen in time;

I love the luminous light within your dark eyes,
living without your love is not really living,
I am sorrowful, as days are like night to me;

Tomorrow at dawn when the grass whitens,
knowing that after the pain, joy will come,
will my love come back again, I wonder;

I swoop into that golden sunshine,
to free myself of grief and melancholy,
to contemplate eternity and my somber life.

CONFUSED SEASONS

Tall undressed trees indiscreet and denuded,
like naked women, having cast off their leafy
endearments,
playful, secret and indistinct, they are;

Summer is finished, they say,
naked branches grasp that still azure sky,
unbeknown to them winter decent, while they shiver;

Where is that golden sun, celebrated by them,
with its fractured lintels of warm air,
no longer can it behold those waxen golden petals;

Glowing in the last wayward rays of the sun,
Leaf's fluttering down, bereft of life,
as the season brutally laughs;

I softly kiss that smooth naked trunk,
of those tall and indistinct trees,
monsieur, I am not, she said;

Yet, her smile was feigned and hidden,
reality seems unbeknown to her,
while winters sunny and gentle kiss will change to a
frozen embrace

FOG

The slowly falling fog is enshrouding the bare gloomy
trees,
now denuded of their leafy garments that was,
grasped and carried away by the winter's callous hand;

Like a white silken sheet flowing over that lonely
stand of trees,
a pearly white veil hiding the trees secrets,
as beaded grasses in the enchanted wood are bending
their luscious heads in pain;

I listen to the chorus of those ethereal birds,
like a dreamlike and tranquil chant,
in this secluded white world;

I pain about the lost chromatism hidden behind those
tranquil waves of white silk,
silently I wait for the cold south wind still playing in
the Nore's valley's,
and as the hoar-frost is falling, my soul spreads out
it's raven wings;

Nothing is sweeter to my pained heart,
as the frozen morning fog after those long dark
winter's nights,
showing anonymous patterns and shapes like eternal
sights;

Seeing those sights contrived by cold,
freeing my soul of those wan feelings that in winter prevail,
forever free and in that bed of chance I sleep.

FROST

The last of the sparse grass has grass whitens during
that dark gloomy night,
the waning sun with her feeble fractured light,
fails to penetrate the gloom;

Winter has arrived holding me in its cruel callous grasp,
I walk in those dark woods bereft of life,
and mull over the blessing once enjoyed;

Nature dies grasped into winter frigid hands,
we see the dying sun with its golden elixir, now gone,
it's chalice of nectar empty and barren;

The bleak future hold hope for us,
as soon, the pure light will return and the fallen
flowers will return,
while we see winter's veiled looks;

Unable to stop time until we reach the bottom of life's
cup,
we will retrieve that flower and perfume that once was,
and listen to her melodious chant still there.

MYSTERY

Coldness is weighing down my heart,
as raindrops plummet upon roofs and on the loamy
ground they flowed,
while the last lark flies 'cross the greying sky singing
its final ode;

The sun gleams with her feeble arrows of fractured light,
we are alone, on that dreamy path,
she and I, our hair soaked, feeling nature's wrath;

Grass dull and lifeless trampled at our feet,
soon love will rise and encompass our soul,
while the saline wind plays with my hair ignoring its
final goal;

Cold air touches that open sea where tides move to
and fro,
forming a surface like a woman's skin soft,
and moving at leisure,
I laugh and endure the torment of that pleasure;

While my soul harbors a mystery,
I want to walk near her, yet not be there,
beside her, and knowing all what we will share;

Daring to ask for nothing, knowing none to receive,
I kissed her hand with devoted care,
dreaming of the dreams we will soon share.

ETERNITY

I breath in the fragrance of life, embracing it,
while I look into that blazing ethereal fire, thinking
melancholic thoughts,
lonely trees and bushes, loaded with sweet fruits are
a memory of the past;

Soon we will sink in that frigid darkness of winter,
having said our last good-byes to the bright summer's
light,
trees tall, slender and vigorous are now naked, denuded
of their foliage;

I see your welcoming heart spread out on the sandy shore,
and your eyes shining with surprising candour,
eyes which shine, like stars in that boundless space;

While beyond the curving beach are all my vexations
and sorrows,
hiding behind that foggy existence of mine, unknown
and unwanted,
as the lark sing's while cresting the rising vapours;

I hide those thoughts, aloof and free, in this dark time,
alas, winter chill is holding me in its cruel callous grasp,
and the sun's hidden orb can only send forth it's last
weak rays;

I fly away from my created surroundings,
rising upwards above the woods, clouds and briny seas,
to grasp that last fractured beam of sunlight, that is
so dear to me.

WINTER'S TIME

I feel that raw air of winter onto my skin,
like an insidious touch of penetrating chill from within,
as I contemplate the cold, intrigued by its icy play,
while the wind plays, making patterns everyway;

The sun is gone into hiding,
but the air is not abiding,
I look onwards towards that roaring sea, wild and full
of wonder,
waves without style or any order;

Gone are those rigid masts in the harbour,
blown asunder while watching its neighbour bending
ever farther,
those stormy seas dark, murky and capped by winter's
veil,
I hide in my shelter save from winters flail;

I pain about those lost times once covered by sunshine,
gone are those colorful fractures sunny lines,
replaced by raw wintery weather flows.

DAWN

Morn' dawn, cool and damp,
as if teardrops condense into that leafy swamp,
glittering beads in sun's first light,
night's flown, it's spirit crushed overnight;

A spicy scent, but honey sweet,
floating, like the golden wheat,
my spirit flees, looking for that unknown scent,
when love awakes, in that early morning torment;

Touching the dew in the early daylight,
it velvety coating giving leaf's that silvery sight,
alas, the rising sun's wings take this beauty,
and the halo of time performs it sorrow duty;

While the day displays its innocence,
and birds cover the sky with diligence,
dew, tender, fickle and wet,
as love is, but not yet.

NIGHT

Darkness touches my face,
as dreams float through my brain with no grace,
coldness prevails in those dreams, full of fear and dread,
I am unable to follow that scary tread;

As time goes on, I walk my lonely path,
waiting for that spring day we once had,
the day that evokes pleasure and gratifying sights,
I want to see that again before it turns into nights;

Before me is the waning sun with its now feeble light,
which I will drink till the last drop, no matter how slight,
its light is fading beautiful and sweet, alas,
this poisoned chalice of honey and bile, I cannot surpass.

Till bottom of life's cup, I drink,
not knowing what the future holds or thinks,
flowers fade, their scent yield to that icy wind,
as the sunlight finally rescind.

SWORD OF TIME

Austere and bleak are those days,
moving into that eternal sea of time with its many
shades of greys,
in that sea of our ages, I will cast my anchor,
and cherish the waves while we revisit for what we
hanker;

As I pass those deep broken rocks,
water smashing against torn sides of the docks,
in those nights we cruised silently,
while the roiling waves waited attentively;

Let us love this transient hour,
to drown in that whirling ocean of love, and not cower,
a sea of love filled with sublime waves,
as the unknown tones echoes to earth's graves;

On that stone I came alone, but cannot linger,
as time follows, pointing to me with her lonely forefinger,
while I speak those solemn words:
"O' time, suspend your blessed and awesome sword".

TIMELESS

Time stops, and it does not care,
In those shared moments, we will shed our single tear,
As love consumes us we do not fear,
while passion will take us, not knowing what we share;

Orchestrated, it is, with sensual colours abound,
alas, storm clouds gathered high above the ground,
obscuring the light of that single pleasurable day,
when obscure memories will come into play;

But in all our fears,
we must accept the many tender tears,
as I dream those fragile dreams,
loaded with emotions, hiding the silent screams;

To relive those moments, I think,
holding us back from that fearful brink,
if I could stop the time,
I would climb that timeless rock and claim it as mine.

LEAF'S

While leaf's floats down with ease and grace,
carried down by the winds, to their final resting place,
colourful with umber they are, burnished and vivid red,
not heeding where they will go and what path they
will tread;

While on her slender white feet, Winter has returned
again,
with slight steps in the darkness, trying to hide, but
it is in vain,
as the sun succumbs to the chilly wintery charm,
his cold intentions are viewed with some alarm;

On that dark, cold and dark forest path,
I walk, sad about winter's sorry wrath,
to watch those forests, fill up with snow,
as the eastern wind blows, my fire aglow;

When I stop at that little house,
in that dark and lovely wood, unseen like a grouse,
seeing the dying sky of the year's darkest day,
I return to the woods and my warm hidden lay.

LITTLE ANGEL

I wait for that stranger,
a precious little angel,
fingers and hands, tiny, as if made of gold,
sleepy emerging from the mother's fold;

Silk-like skin showing a shiver,
lips and body, wrapped up, show a little quiver,
platinum colour is the hair,
I cannot do anything but stare;

Little fingers reach out, but never touch,
although I am sure they reach out soon, as such,
crying strong and firm,
showing its need to reaffirm;

There are many things to learn,
as mother's hold is strong and oft stern,
a beautiful child so deep in sleep,
an angel who we do not really want to hear weep.

WORDS

In that halo of mist, light dies,
leaving that sorrow day behind me, which seems wise,
skies filled with wings of those fleeing birds,
barely visible during that nocturnal darkness time;

As a wild salty sea gyrates, with its tidal floods,
unable to find those soft sandy beds that once was
water's life and blood,
ships filled the surface of those beguiled sea,
as hunters hide away on his rocky lee;

In that universal universe of ours, light has died,
a broken shadow gone, as it did not abide,
my words are gone now, to watch that rough sea,
something I admire, as all my words flee;

That shadow was broken, because of me,
it will think it over, it said, with a certain glee,
while I hunt for my shadow,
I write all those final words, I still know.

SOUNDS

Among the stars and among the many moons,
that haunt the seas and the hidden shores,
we know there is still time for sunlight,
as the wild waves crash and die within their spume;

I see that arc of the sky,
I write this as I breath in that scent of those dying waves,
waves forgotten and a sky whose colour will soon falls,
I cannot keep pace with the change of those nuances;

Am I one of those blind witnesses,
gliding faceless among those dying waves,
seeking the song of youth, that once was,
listening to seashells to capture its last echo;

I set a course towards that fading sound,
with the fish living among those waves,
in that colourless world of different moons,
while I dream in the dark bed of winter.

WINTER SUN

Winter's first day, sun stretched taut and low,
its light bloodstained and golden,
dark clouds approach filled with promise and terror,
as the universe awaits the flowering of winter;

We follow the bank of the river downstream,
through the empty and barren plain,
seeing those frozen skeletal plant remains,
of last summer's blooms;

All we have left is a memory, of the summer's
flowering rose,
while the night swoops in like a vulture,
stealing the final light of that blood-filled sun,
as I wait on that venomous meadow for the coming
winter;

Autumn now past, diseased and dying,
storms rip through the weeping forest,
ripe fruit has now fallen, but no one's culls,
snow covering my memories, of last season's murmurs.

TWILIGHT

Silently stars drop toward the horizon,
glistening jewels disappearing behind that bare picket
of trees, that
is darker than the angry sky.
The forest is a deep void, swallowing, that endless stream
of gleaming stones, taken by those bare and silent trees;

At twilight some stars never move,
too tired from their journey thought the universe,
they sit and wait for things that are not there,
timid and shy, staying far out in their own dust,
lost and lonely they are;

But the self-assured planets move with great presence,
travelling confidently across that that dark sky,
ignoring the lost orphans,
carving their own paths through the star studded sky,
I look upward and I feel lost,
unable to reach that never-ending horizon,
and to see that river of the night.

TIME OF YEAR (SONNET)

This time of year, when it's wet and foggy,
wet yellow leaves have dropped, or some, I would say
as the bare forest guards itself, against the wintery cold,
summer is just a fleeting memory of sunny events past;

Skies dark and wild, decent upon those trees,
light's faded, taken by the power of the earth,
as nature plunges into that ice abyss of frost.
and the ashes of time follow that lonely sad road;

In that barren meadow, I stood, on what was once mine.
I am consumed by grief at moon's departure of now,
darkness and sadness cover night's heart,
consumed by what was once nourishing;

Thus, I breath, bringing that dying fire aglow,
and treasure that fragment of summer's dream.

THE TRAVELLER

A path split two, into that picket low,
perhaps I should follow left, despite the snow,
as I had travelled far, I waited as I did not know,
searching for that answer, in that winters throe,
one path was bare and without past, there I should go;

But the other perhaps safer still,
would it lead me to those chilly waters downhill?
having taken a path not knowing where,
snow covered leaves, red, umber and fair,
this will it lead me to those waters cold and clear;

On that morning when I walked that path unclear,
filled with white snow, I did fear,
yet knowing it will lead me those shores so dear,
across that river flowing near,
not doubting that path would lead me there.

DIFFERENCES

Ebb and flood are timeless, they say,
during the decay of a flood, when
the moon has not yet set,
I will cast out my nets in that promising bay,
filled with hope, are those nets, and not yet wet,
as I watch those sinking silver cords,
thinking how hard and unkind
we were when we fought,
now with calloused hands I hold my nets,
against the wooden ship's boards,
as I think again of my those last cruel words.

MY QUEEN

The sun has barely dried that morn's dew
flocks were looking for shade along the dark hedges,
as I wait for my queen, as glass, and brittle, she is,
a lily, pale and fair, softer than beeswax in the warm
daytime,
her lips seizing me with pleasure,
and in that inmost delight I do sink, without succor;

Along that cool and rushing brook, I dream,
however, I think, bad is best,
but I remember, excellent is neither
my queen, so fair and so sweet, she seems,
I did not seek any favours or looks in his eyes,
but she can win my heart, but will she try?

Sad this beauty without pain, but lost for me,
a withered flower, I threw with sadness,
I wonder what I did wrong,
now lost is this portrait that I created, painted that
pain and lost.

BEAUTY

Beauty, vain and brittle, a shine that fades too quickly,
as flowers whither, without care,
lost within that hour of neglect,
beauty seen through windows of twisted metal,

Distorted and misdirected,
but beauty, vain, will spring and yearly grow anew,
can you steal beauty and call it theft, I wonder,
time has flown, my beauty,

I will recall your touch and caress,
living in your universe of radiant suns and soft moonlight,
those blissful moments as I steal your kiss,
beauty that makes, young man cry and old men weep,

Foolish, as gentle rain will become a rage,
and soft sunlight will disappear, behind those soft
gentle clouds,
I wander on those clouds that float across vales and
rocky shores,
they are my host, as we float o'er lakes and trees,

While beauty fades on my inward eyes.

AMOUR

Love young and innocent has no conscience,
but is conscience needed for love to have options?
love 's as spring grows, and matures,
'tis a spirit growing, like my fire aglow,
I wonder, as it's walks in beauty;

Filling those cloudless skies and starry nights with warmth,
feeling good in darkness and all that is bright,
fair is that love as sweet music and poetry join,
and agree together in love;

Love a triumphal price to be won,
a price heavenly, never to be hidden,
it's melodious discords of its past now forgotten.

FEAR

Upon midnight during that night so dreary,
I pondered, weak and weary,
I do remember th't bleak December day,
'twas cold and gray, as they say,
I hear that gentle tapp'ng,
quietly, I looked up, like a mouse caught napp'ng;

Sparks jumping out from the burn'ng embers, all about.
as if pleasure was abounding with'n that fire of mine,
does it know the visitor, I thought with ire.
while the gyrating winds whip up that saline sea,
and tides scour the'r own beds with glee;

A visitor, I thought, no doubt,
when I opened the door of my chamb'r to see.
a lady stood there, a stranger,
patient she was, like a spid'r, unaware of any danger,
silken stings encircled my soul, and I
felt terror as never felt before,

It's tread engulfs me, I was awestruck
wh't what she had in store;
my soul grew stronger, overcoming my dread,
waking up from my dream, not
knowing where' it would lead,
ignoring those gossamer threads
surrounding me, as I woke,

The stranger has released me, her
love spell left like smoke.

TIME

As time moves on and the brave daylight seeks his
hideous nightly bed,
I behold those faded flowers well past their prime,
mature trees now leafless, denuded and bare are wilting,
as summer's green is all but gone,
stolen by autumn's greedy hand;

But now that autumn is borne away, by that white
chilly one,
among the wastes of time, this year's autumn is gone
awry,
like a woman's portrait painted by nature's hand,
hue of hues, unknown by anyone,
now winter is here, stealing that woman's soul;

Whereupon it looks and I am,
worried about April's first born flowers.
sun's glorious eye look'd on at winter's horrid crime,
the plunder of woman's summer soul's,
once, that winter was a fair sweet youth;

Gone are those days, as winter's is showing no remorse,
as souls lost, seldom or never found again,
winter's crime, like broken glass no cement can redress,
flowers withered, covered by winters snowy shame.

CHILDREN

I see their hope, and glitter from afar,
a bright and fruitful valley, full of stars it is,
from which that child is born, and appears, without wars;

I lie on this bed of childbirth,
uncontrolled and I tremble of dread, as it is without mirth,
a feeling of nearn'ss and dead, I feel,

Not the joy of giving birth, as I was promised when we
wed, as I know little or no facts of this matter,
why does it not make sense, about which way they prattle,

Knowledge is not the truth, they say,
experience belongs to ways past, without affray,
I am on my own now, totally and utterly alone,

I lie back driving outwards from my inwards that has
grown,
the sun goes pale, and the moon has set,
as I fall into that world full of bitter words, not knowing
what will happen yet,

I am calm and silent, controlled, and called ma'am,
but I am alone and alone I am.

But as you hear the murmur, and my deep intense hum,
you will know, that I am glad to be a mum.

DREAM TIMES (SONNET)

Just as summer's sun dried that dewy morn,
and night shut its weary and shady eye,
I wake before the evenings echo fades,
and my skin feels harsh and so cold;

Still trying to defend that challenging cup,
while I am lying in that summer's grass,
In the new world, dreaming of thing to come,
as a new moon awakens from its dark bed;

Leafless trees are confined to their doom,
my peace shattered by that darkness and gloom,
my own fears, surrounding my simple soul,
forfeited to that threatening doom, it is;
can I still find that fresh and true love,
mortal and spirited as I did subscribe.

WORDS (SONNET)

Those words I have written with no strain,
not passing judgment nor reason or pain,
as my fire burns in its cauldron firmly aglow,
my skin still cold and clammy from winters show;

Speech and reason do not alter winters grip,
I wait for warm climes to finish their yearly trip,
as that waning moon goes towards its nightly bed,
and once I was certain of the uncertain time ahead;

Now time has blurred my vision again,
gone is that sacred beauty, treasured in vain,
that flame that burns brighter than then all,
I fear time h's altered my vision, thus my downfall.
   Love grows with time and care, they say,
   yet will it blossom in winter's icy sway.

PROMISES (SONNET)

Your eyes, yes, they pity me, but are filled with love,
they torment me with fury and distain,
I mourn those moments, full of sorrow and pain,
as stars and the moon blossom in the nightly sky;

Clouds appear above that horizon, dark ahead,
like dark cheeks peeking above world's edge,
clouds full of false promises unbeknown to me,
without those red lips so beloved and full;

I have seen those roses red and snowy white,
roses that will not survive those unkind days,
those perfumes, full of promising delight,
like music that I hear in my tormented heart.
        As I remember those summer's nights past,
        full of promises and soft moonlight aglow.

WALKS

Time, as I in walk in those gyrating winds,
I see that distant edge of the horizon,
sand blowing, nearly unseen in that driving rain,

Grains floating, moving forward in that unending rain,
like boats moving, their sails propelled by the wind,
as the sun sets beyond dark horizon.

Hills obscured by dark clouds at that horizon,
angry clouds stocked with that promised rain,
pushed onwards by that never-ending wind.

Rain carried by that wind, driven in from that unseen
horizon.

SOUVENIRS

I look towards that tranquil water surface,
into that ethereal liquid darkness,
not seeing the chaos below that smooth shoal.
I scarcely understand that ocean of ages,
to cast an anchor for one day or more.

Behold, I came alone, not to linger,
To remember that nights as we wandered silently,
onto that unmoving glassy surface.
Thinking of April's first-born flowers,
amid other things so rare.

Duty called so great, but with a wit as poor as mine,
I do not witness the change of seasons,
neither do I distinguish the guiding stars.
Am I debarr'd the betterment of peace,
to make my daily grief length longer?

Time, suspend your flight, delay your hours.
Alas, my thought fragmented, by duty is vague,
and all those friends which I though buried,
life filled with faults and even I in this,
But, are you my advocate, to plea my peace?

I am not lame, deprived nor despis'd,
I look what is best this is that I have,
to entertain the time with thoughts of love,
I commit those petty wrongs that my liberty allows,
While I mourn my art and straying youth.

Silence falls as curfew announced sun's waning way,
the ploughman travels home, the end of its working day,
and the cattle slowly following the well-trodden pathway,
Light fades, hiding the once glimmering fields in grey.

Gone, are those droning beetles following sun's glossy
light,
the owl mopes in the forest, bereaved of its nightly right,
of such, as I wander to that hidden heath in moonlight,
beneath those mossy elms, and the solemn stillness
of night,

Left behind the days warmth as I lay, in spite of morn's
coming,
ignoring that muddy rill, which I saw in daylight.

MORNING (SONNET)

One morn I miss her on my custom's hill,
along the heath that's near her favorite tree;
she might well come yet, there beside the rill,
she wasn't up the lawn, or wood's dark lee;

End of day, curfew tolls it's starting way,
fading's sun glimmering view's, drowns from day's sight;
will, I not cast a lingering look at day's fray?
gone, as bees, in their wheeling droning flights;

Beneath the oaks and gentle birch, I wait;
as I am tired of my wander's ways,
waiting for morn's rooster's shrill rowdy fete,
and the breezy incense-breathing mooring's rays;

      Gone is night's owl answer to the moon's call;
      no more shall I rise from my solitary fall.

END OF SUMMER (SONNET)

As summer's air touch the last sweet warm corn,
and chiding autumn, is to be here soon,
one by one petals drop while summer' mourn,
cooing cause 'twere no cloud to hide the moon.

Gone are the butterflies I use to chase,
I see the fall of golden leaves sheltering weeds,
and plants are dying with colour and grace,
while birds still hunt the last summer' ripe seeds.

As the last of those shiny 'noon's, cloud gather,
and rain wets my sunbeaten summers face,
while the aged sun lulling hand makes me swoon,
and summer warm air hides with no trace,

> Will I have to ransom autumn's beauty?
> and reveal the winters chill hidden booty?

NIGHT DREAMS

Love, as roses are alluring, her rose-briars will hurt,
the wild rose blossom's in this early spring,
its briars protecting her from her sure fall;

a delicate flower that send forth its profound scent,
in that sunny green vale, I lay,
thinking of love, as birds carolled joyfully;

while there, I took my her heart to me,
wondering about all those bright things to be,
when winter's time is here, all will vanish;

then my visions will be in vain,
but as earth echo's ends,
and winter's naked tomb is there;

love will cease like a night's dreams, floating away,
leaving me with that rose scent, and my creation true;
and thinking of the briar's hurt.

ARRIVAL

To arrive during a blue summer's eve in a fruitful land,
I love it's, want for sun, pain and life not planned;

I wander its paths and smell its freshness,
say nothing at all thinking would be reckless;

Its love and desire to sing of joy, and know it is rude,
for in my crazed life, I see that;

That one, I vowed to live without mistress,
the mistress of sun and pallor and pain,

Only to love, live and enjoy that day,
to mix, as each have our bliss again;

To deck your fortune with virtuous deeds,
while summer's greens are all girded up;

My voice will rise, be heard anew,
and will resist those painful sobs and sighs;

And keep loving, after having so loved.

ROMANCES

When the ragged winter's hand has defaced autumn's
mask,
and I look at those dark pools where the stars still sleep,
I see the drifting veils that waves softly efface,
whispering romances for the breeze t' keep;

Nestling fledging's beating their wings in darkness nigh,
far away mad seas billowing and roaring their fury high;
as I dash out from under that starlit sphere,
your heart will hear my song 'f nature's fear;

While in trees yonder' I lament in that night,
my eyes focus on my wisdom, without delight,
accepting my folly, for which I didn't crave,
alas, autumn is here, harsh, to summers lave;

As the sun drowns in its own blood without distress,
and flowers loveliness evaporates like a hair' tress,
how beautiful and radiant those sunbursts were,
and those eves lit by glowing embers, with her.

MEN

A woman's heart gentle and so unknown,
a mistress adept, but imperfect, they say,
with shifting change her treasure is shown,
not adding purpose to nothing but decay;

We plead for their love and maybe some glory,
then we rest and forget for which we toiled,
after the victory, we will tell the story,
not worried into what we are embroil'd;

As a warrior unbeknown and no quests,
the gilded object and things treasured rare,
wishing me to fight for one I like best,
for sweet love rememb'red, wealth, trust s' fair,

It's that beauty I'm tempting her, with glee,
from me far off, while others near, will flee.

END OF AUTUMN

During many a glorious October morning's that I have
seen,
silently, as yellowing leaves ripen and drop,
often this autumn's golden glow, that's dimm'd;

And summer's lease, too short and fierce,
night's wild wind died after taken many a late bud,
tomorrow's waste and nature's bounty;

Morning's hours are slow to form,
but nature's course is untrimmed and fair,
the sun enchanting in that gentle mist;

I pick the last of my ripe fruit soft and round it's,
as I kiss the golden face in the meadows now gone,
tomorrow they may reform or will go burned by frost.

MEDITATION (SONNET)

I am at peace with my sorrows: hush we smile.
no, don't want to drink from that poisoned cup,
filled with waters deep, of regret, nectar and bile,
walk that single path, with dreamlike steps up.

The cup will not persuade me that I am old,
as I see the furrows of life, like love,
and answers where not yet, for me, inscrolled,
I wait and look at what I am write of.

So, for fear or trust I must recompense,
am that warrior, fighting for pride hidden?
I do not have skill or words of eloquence,
lost, after the victory once unbidden.

> They watch with cunning eyes, and dare to boast,
> a sweet thief, that steals joy and honour most.

STORM (SONNET)

I stand in that hot ring alone and bitter,
waiting for my fate with no fear or doubt,
the soft ground grips my feet as I speed hither,
searching for a path and avoid this bout;

Crowds run fast to escape my pounding feet,
falling, jumping climbing to avoid sharp horns,
fear filled eyes, pound'ng hearts in beat,
red and white are in his sight like ugly thorns;

The bull unaware of what has transpir'd,
the matador sword ready, it's stance firm and lithe
look'ng for that soft shoulder spot so desir'd,
that bright red cape provocative, as it writhes;

Down strikes the searing steel to enter its flesh,
ending the bulls rage, and love, that hidden mesh.

WINTER (SONNET)

Walk lightly, as they are so very near,
there well hidden under those golden leaves,
be silent, watch your step, as they can hear,
those late flowers, still hidden in quiet sheaves;

As my eye and heart are in mortal fight,
I will lose that quest of beauty and time,
hdden beauty smother'd and touched by that cold blight,
flowers, summer's beauty, killed in them prime;

They were hardly known, with many days to grow,
soon, they will not hear nor see your gold'n hair,
they were young and fair, just like coming snow,
picked off by wind and winter's cold stare;

I cannot rest while vexing their cold end,
as I die, yes, oppress'd with melancholy.

AUTUMN'S FIGHT

They tell me she's charm'ng,
that autumn, as I do not see her infernal secrets,
her lullaby, her hands and the long slumber that's
disarming,
as winter's blanket will slowly cover and makes us equal;

My spirit once had love but this day now, at this tired
struggle,
the love of my life gave his fatal stroke,
goodbye, welcome, crime, horror and winter's tussle,
my love, passion and hope for the flowers, soon to
die, broke;

is not you, autumn with sun so clear and so white,
yes, in me you see the twilight of such a day,
my so very white summer's flowers soon dying of blight,
I hate passion and the spite of it makes me hurt with'n
your latest ray;

      Like the seasons, as they are yearly new and old,
      so is my love still telling me what has been told.

HER PROTEST

My love, she is fair, mild but so fickle,
a woman in this world I live in now,
softer than melting wax, a lily, but brittle,
with damask dye to grace her private vow;

Brighter than crystal glass and yet as frail,
her lips and mine are joined so often now,
she foiled me framed love not to fail,
her faith, her oaths, and her tears, still raw;

Yet, in the midst of all of her protest,
she burns with love, do I to trust my eyes?
dreading to lose the love, for which I guessed,
the truth I shall not know, neither the ties;

Not daring to wake, as she seizes my lips,
to kiss and hold me till she ends her grips.

WINTER'S DAY

During those gentle hours of work, I wait,
for winters paradise to start his show,
lifting my existence and rise up straight,
I will not lie dormant or melt like snow;

And wait under that wan light of winter,
I end work to dance, writhe, for no reason,
being in heaven, as cold days splinter,
a winter's day might seem short, this season;

We remember, as summer distillations are gone,
leaving debris and mayhem in its wake,
it's beauty bereft and days now badly drawn,
winter's tyranny looking at summer's take;

Cold and unfair, cunning in what it does,
me, a prisoner pent up into that icy grip.

RECEIVING NOTHING

Will love take root again in my very soul, I wonder,
will, I be touched by that flaming fire, so wanted,
I was cut and wounded once, blooded red, like
flowering roses,
scars visible, but not seen, deep hidden cellars of grief;

But yes, I will admire the stars in that orb of darkness,
attain those heights of passion, renewed and desired,
alas, is it a false loveliness, disguised by that face of
amour,
or, will I walk those grassy dales with her, yet unnoticed;

Asking for nothing and receiving nothing,
will she read my verses as I write, dreaming them,
let our mouths kiss, embrace, and sweeten our life,
and with half closed lips declare your love to me;

On those warm summer's eves we will cross those
sunbeams,
dreaming, as we smell the freshness of newly cut grass,
we say nothing, to break that sweet sacred spell,
and, our love will rise to fill our very souls;

END OF SUMMER

Silently the sun rises out of its nightly slumber,
shadows hide, awaiting sun's fierce look,
veils of mist rise to join their brethren,
hiding the tree's peaks, soon to be painted golden by
the morning's light;

The last of that misty membrane is drifting not
knowing where to go,
will it join the umbra, that is still hiding in the dells,
birds chase and sing on that now blond plain filled
with golden spots,
but their fun and adventure is soon to end;

The rising sun looking disapproving at natures play,
knowing that this too will have to end soon,
flowers turn to promising brightness, hoping for light
and warmth to come,
slowly nature follows sun's vivid controlling rules;

Crowds of darkness are chased like beggars away
from those likely spots,
I follow my golden path home, near that vale and
shadows dark,
to rest from my nightly toil, disapproving of nature's
warm play;

As autumn looks on guilty and silently,
at the approaching end of summer's days.

LOVE THAT SUMMER (SONNET)

That time of the year, as none, is here now,
golden leaves fly, but some or few will hang,
while those cold weath'red boughs shudder and bow,
sun is fading fast on last summer's rang.

The ripe'ng crop has seen its last dusk,
though to itself it only lived once and die,
darkness falls and the black night seals day's husk,
sun's on her death-bed won'dring, gone and why.

Leaves, consumed of which it was nourish'd by,
as late, the birds sang their song in twilight,
now, they do not inherit the nest they lie,
unmoved, cold, as no temptation might.

      This how, it's makes my love more strong,
      to love that summer for which I must long.

FRANCE (SONNET)

Yellowing foliage and that dying grass,
the sight of winter as't besieg's your face,
we wonder when that frigid beauty will pass,
will it come and go without it's cold trace;

The dark colour of the rain, like blood spill'd,
dark as the French's past, now gone and wash'd,
in those trenches and fields fill'd with those killed,
I will ask why, that field's beauty was squash'd;

unbeknown to me in French history past,
I must greet those barons in their proud liv'ry,
and the youths who gazed on as none asked,
and all of lusty days are lost without victory;

      I do not count and make an old excuse,
      or worry about shame, nor thriftless 'cuse

BEAUTIFUL

My love, rest you tired eyes,
as I watch your languid pose,
you, my fountain of pleasure and guile,
continues as passion reigns.

While rain washes those leaves,
still young and so vibrant green,
floating, moving and never resting,
that fountain of warm passion.

A dream of fire and love,
of you, whom the night enhances,
endless as rain is pouring down,
is it caused by the that love?

Desires felt, and hopes so long in vain,
as our souls are blended by love deep,
kind but not cruel, as my love is joining me,
my heart is tortured by that arrow of love.

LOST LOVE

Isolation, I'm lost in a nostalgic mist that surrounds me,
confined by her, I do not hear,
a pool of thoughts that separates your soul.
the fingers of the dazzling heat of my body is seeking,
I love to probe and burn;

I burn and I drown, immersed in my thoughts,
dream of silence and secret pleasures hidden for the
moment.
yes, I will walk with my eyes fixed on my thoughts,
without seeing anything outside, without noise,
alone, unknown, hands crossed,
sad, and the day for me will be like the night;

Alone, I will not look at the evening gold,
neither sails in the distance descending from the coast,
and when I get there, I'll put on my grave,
a bouquet of white flowers,
this is love, sacrificing everything without hope of return

SETTING SUN (SONNET)

That orb of the even'ng sun set in clouds,
and storms have entered that sombre nightly shroud,
over golden streamlets, and forests all around,
the dy'ng day hidden behind sun's golden mound.

So is that beauty which I hold in lease,
beauty, full of candor and doesn't ever cease,
while I bend and I lower my sight and head,
and worship your gay smiles, gentle, as is said.

Unmiss'd by it's creation, joyous and vast,
still chill'd in the light, soon, as it is cast,
will that beauty die and her guileless heart?
leaving me enslav'd, as 't was at the start.

> Fortune; chances of where my soul is lost
> While I roam through life, count'ng the final cost.

WINE

I bring unknown wine to my lips long parch'ng,
and summon them to drink that ruby juice.
my hands hug that cooling translucent glass,
promis'd heaven, yet it does not reach closely.

Hope, that subtle glutton, it feeds upon the fair,
I wait by that eternal gate of sweetn'ss,
knowing it will not come to my mort'l side,
angels must have seen my desire and hope.

Resting in the land of viands and wines,
I did not know the ample bread of lands,
some good some poor like fruit of mountain bush,
it was so unlike the drop I tasted last.

The birds and I me have often shared,
in nature's joyous enticing dining-room.

SUMMER TIME PAST

Amid the hush'd rustle of those plant'd hills,
abounding life fed by that watery spill,
the sweetness I longed for night and day,
alas, not a garden where the peacock strays.

An anci'nt bridge and delicate crumbly terraces,
a garden with level lawns and old carriages ,
buildings design from a haughtier age, past
and the horizon fades and shad's are cast.

Sur'ly among a man's green lawns love is found,
dark summers nights with candl's and no bird's sound.
before indiffer'nt stone gard'n deities I wait,
for the gentleness none there could ever create.

A house that is shelter'd by acres of ground,
and grey stone fireplaces heat'ng that rooms I found.

STONE WALL

My own secret meditation and thoughts,
are lost amidst that labyrinth of winter's air,
gone is what I made in art or politics,
old ancient political habits stick fast, I know.

Like snow sticks to that jagg'd stony wall,
melting and wan'ng in the young spring's breath,
whatever mischief I creat'd let's not mock the worthy,
I will not lift my hand, maybe, to help the precious,
wise and none.

As winter closes in, we call on spring to come forth,
hoping the abounding hedges will soar up,
declaring winter's gone and spring's ascents,
let that new face of spring, rove that dark garden.

> I wait till morn'ng meal arrives, I do,
> waiting on a woman's knee of flesh and bone.

THOUGHTS

Heaven and peace are places I can't reach,
and like fruit that matures on a tree, I desire one of each,
tantalizing me, but they hopelessly hang,
drowning, sinking to their abhorrent abode, from
which they came,

If mortal lips could divine and deliver that single silent
syllable,
will I get that fruit, hanging from that azure sky,
unreachable,
our statures reach for the sky, and we fear,
daily our heroism we recite, but we don't come near,

I offer you, that love is life, and life is immortality,
follow that brook into your heart, where blushing birds
drink without formality,
alas, will shadows tremble of those little draughts,
you pry,
less be aware, or that brook of life will soon burn and
be dry,

> And when time's up, there will be no love,
> as nothing has ever been erased, but changed
> as a raven or a dove.

DECEMBER DAY

During the dark hours, that gentle work flows,
I gather my thoughts,
but that hideous winter, and hate confounds me,
as the rising tree sap is checked by frost,
and lusty green leafs are gone now;

Beauty of snow that covers the baren'ss everywhere,
is it fear that will wet that widow's eye's,
or is it wisdom and beauty, I wonder,
so should that beauty which you hold in lease;

Protect you against the stormy gusts of winter's day,
and the bare rage of death's eternal cold,
while the sun, as is common, went abroad,
and the flowers, accustomed, blew away;

No soul has passed solstic' this time,
to make all things anew.

LAST BIT OF SUMMER

The sun rose, on its usual time,
a ribbon of events, dark all new.
that endl'ss time and dawn sublime,
sun's fingers brush the azure sky so blue.

Full of hope and grace,
I crave for that summer's light,
rising up round that old'n stone vase,
flirting with that green leaflet so slight.

These are days when skies aren't rich,
coloured purple and gold by mistake,
it will not cheat the birds colour on that ridge,
as the berry's cheeks are plumb when awake.

As days shorten, unbeknown to them,
autumn colours will engulf that wooden diadem.

HOPE

As wind that blew down the forested slope,
I cours'd uncaring trough those dim wood'n hollows,
past the rocks that up rear, unable to cope,
and the murmuring river fall, I can follow;

Past the grove's dreamy hush, in noonday's heat,
her charm would lead to the bower she has made,
whereon the days of woe's, those I can't beat,
foreshadowed it was, in that glade I strayed;

can I compare her to those summer's day,
as rough winds do shake daring buds in May,
and summer's lease is far too short, to lay,
in those eternal lines of time, loves will stray;

> Alas, as long I can breath and eyes can see,
> I live on in hope to gives life to you.

FRIENDSHIP

As we sat on that meadow warm and green,
talking trough the dark night, a never ending stream,
O' what an expression in that broiling night,
as if we had all summer's time, we might.

For it is natural to live in memory,
alone I nurse the earth with reverie,
she smiled and that changed me, that night
I have tried many things and nothing despite.

Friendship never ends, and true faith discovered was
I laid my hand there 'in as is done, because,
in this troubled world I am unfair and blind,
and those candles I light as they are there.

Within my solitary soul she's enshrined
that child of celestial birth, I could say.

SWEET MUSIC

As I sat in that tranquil meadow sweet,
under those branches covering the darkening sky,
I felt that solemn silence at our first meet,
amidst the languor's of those trees trunks nearby.

the lowering sky is ominous and mean
as the moon stares though those rare cloud's gaps,
and that narrow wind complains that's it hasn't been,
then amidst fading light, we see winter lapse,

But winter's saved in his alabaster chamber,
as pink clouds float like those listless pheasants,
who feel the air but not trust their flying wings,
fields degrade in winters ice that's still reigns.

I bowed to those birds that sang sweet music,
as the sun sank down dressed in that golden tunic.

PAIN

The look of agony, the truth etched on,
it is not possible' to feign 'n sunset,
time's is overlooking it, before dawn's gone
within lives wisdom, beauty, and what's beset;

We watch that clock that has told us the time,
and have seen that day sink in its somber' night,
like lofty trees bare, dark and full 'f grime,
then time's beauty, I question, is so slight;

Since sweets and beauties do themselves no gain,
and die faster than earl' fields grow in pain,
in that waste of that time we'll see nature's lease,
battling against stormy gusts of winter's frigid increase;

> The end is truth's and fails beauty's spring
> bloom,
> I can't fight for love to stop time's impending
> doom.

SUNSET

While I dwell in those deep caves of stone,
crowned by their bare majestic stony peaks,
I live in exalted calmness amidst of darkness,
as this azure splendour of the shore, I seek;

While' I dwell in those deep caves of stone,
the billowing sky 's depicted dark and grim,
but in a mystical way kindness is shown,
and sun-set colours show on that rocky trim;

While I dwell in that deep cave of stone,
the sun's eye swoon at those steep stone peaks,
as I ask the fading solar queen to 'tone,
to catch at least one last ray before they fail,

Now night makes firm her dark lonely domain,
following my faint steps on the marsh's rim
of pain.

A MELANCHOLIC YEAR

As night approaches and sunset drowns still,
the flowers in autumn, evaporate and die,
a melancholic yearly dance repeated time over time,
music and chaos will appear, vast and forever;

After summers warmth, roiling skies turn to earth,
and the wailing of nature's scent is drowned,
just like earth stills and forests drown deeply,
sweet souls unable to face the future so divine,

The dark moon of all the world is weary,
even his lilied bed can become nature's tomb,
as winter approaches and the dance ends,
music and chaos will appear vast and forever;

And sun dies within her blood-red brine,
the sage will take his red essays in vain,
unable to see chaos and stillness of earth,
just like earth stills and forests drown deeply.

MAGIC

O' mage unknown, whose power assist my art,
as I light that flame of nature's fear of dead,
heaven's cold hidden, corpses loved of old,
behold, there at shores where celestials die;

You who makes them a Midas, seeing my art
of that most clever alchemist, makes life
for this through it might turn my gold in iron
let heaven hold, as hell has many to spare;

During this witching night, that's criminal's ally,
we have toiled today! Yes, bring solace
and the night, that brings souls and woes 'unknown,
while light flickers in windows still not known;

As with folk with many a care and, soaring,
dash their heads on walls or blind of caring,
as the sky slowly closing every giant door,
and man, the rebel, turns a beast once more.

DEMONS

That once golden, but now grey, ashen land,
lit by that pensive full moon, partly bann'd;
a world full of cruel and curious demons,
spirits with unhappy eyes for no reasons;

Out of my tower, with chin upon my hands,
I'll watch the sad and whispering human bands;
and softly, through the mist, lit by moon's light,
seeing lofty pride, but I knew demons weren't right;

Is 't not that I pity those empty and cold mind,
insensible to mortal grief with eyes unkind;
the moon tries to pour pale enchantment light,
and people return home unknown of demon plight;

> And in my thoughts, it's in that sad place apart,
> I dream of eagles, and demons with no heart.

DESIRE

I set forth with my thoughts aflame again,
how vast the world is, while that moonlight reigns,
it's equal to the child's desire to play,
as I cradle' that song of waves and bays;

I do not flee the memory of childhood,
neither do I hide from surges, I should,
infinity on the finite sea of changing words,
I'm the voyager, with tales of fights and swords;

Within my dim sea-weary eyes you can read,
I can't travel without sail or rudder, as said,
can I stop the water's weary flood tides?
and still discover enchanted cities besides;

> Dreaming of that paradise of my own desire,
> desires no mortal man can give me.

TIME

Those lost sea-beaches have seen many a war,
hope and fear, sunsets after many a sorrow spree,
far away the sun sinks over that distant town,
by fate or chance created from gyrating clouds;

Tree bark will thicken as the years pass by,
arduous branches will rise to the sky,
showing the strange wild loveliness desired,
and we are always sorrowful but so proud;

I have seen many of those jewels covered thrones,
in the palaces filled with pomp and gleam,
where fighters rest from the weary battle front,
in robes and a madness to the eyes;

> The world says our age is little and too vain,
> hoping that the grim time, is an eager foe;

AUTUMN FADES

The air so somber, envelopes that old town,
bringing peace to some and others who drown,
as mist like a long sheet is dragged along,
the seasons will pass till autumn fades strong;

Drawing the sun out of my heart, from summer's past,
then comes winter with his weary snowy blasts,
and gardens where marble fountains are asleep,
there I build my castle against that dark cold sweep;

I will not need her with her stealthy tread,
it can plunge me deep in pleasures ahead,
sinless hope built on senseless words of hope,
then I will dream of horizons deep and far;

> The seasons will pass till autumn fades strong
> smiling, floating in water where they belong;

CHARM

Yes, I am a leaf blown by that strong wind,
and sleep on the gale's breast that I can find,
that pendulous cradle forever moving forwards,
waves placid movement that follows shore's foam borders;

I wait for morn's balmy kiss promised with haste,
will, I catch the sweet breath of that rose, so wasted,
walking past mountains, and grove's dreamy hush,
thro' the glens and the valleys clear and lush;

Around me the breeze and leaves are dancing,
while the dewdrops upon me would be glancing,
in the roseate glow of that morn's crushing light,
I would find that matching leaf, gold and slight;

       Yes, I would fly, till a charm stopped my way,
       that charm that would lead to that promised lay.

AUTUMN'S FINISHED

In that azure sky, scentless and naked,
I see that once golden cornfield now vacated,
As a stately abbey rears its dome over her shrine,
oft blundering bees, deceived, by that old golden line;

Come buzzing to my side, I feel the sting,
like morn's first sunbeam piercing during new spring,
As those mountains old, whose brow's white and cold,
guarding that field next to the sky, once gold,

The awakening sun asked where all that beauty's gone,
I answer with sunken shame, and hope not shone;
With all the treasure of lusty days now finished,
summer's golden corn field needs has diminished;

Autumn needs are a different golden colour,
a tinge more tranquil and much of a pallor.

SNOW

White snow like a clean sheet dropping onto its bed,
a land buried under white blankness,
time vanish in that white veil,
nature is buried in that noiseless drift;

I step out in that white world of softness,
and shake that snow-covered branch,
then drifting snowflakes obscure colour,
making me a willing prisoner in that colourless world;

Worlds yearly fall under its spell,
trees hide under that sheet of nothing,
a snowy mantle, an unsullied covering,
I see all that's there, while admiring nature's calm.

TREMBLING HEART

The sun, an explosion of light that greets us from above,
I see that flower, the furrow, and glade,
that glorious azure skyline, so beloved,
o', happy is he who can hail her love,
more glorious far, than what I dream;

Let us haste to the glade, 'tis late, let us run,
alas, that summer, has eludes me, and I chased it in vain,
the night, irresistible, and its domain dark and sinister,
dreamily admiring my beloved beauty in bizarre delight,
I cannot find these white roses as promised once;

Summers eyes would gaze upon me as if outworn by age,
but fair is the sun when first appear in flames from above,
I have seen her the sun's eye's, swooning with
trembling heart,
but, night falls as gloom and terrors glide in at sun's pass,
bruising that cold unseen terror, that hides in night's
domain.

NIGHT

The sky's slowly closing, like a giant door,
night bring my woes closer and slow memories unknown,

As bells pierce that pall of grey misty air,
it's bitter joy as memories echo over that lake of blood

once lit by that flaming sun, now I sit in the shade of
those sombre yews
watching the fading sunset rays as that red face sinks,

And the darkness devours that last warm rays,
silent owls sit in that dark forest ready to start their call.

From out of that a mountainous furnace, now dark
and hidd'n,
grains of sparkling gold came, as fine as sand,   mystic
in my eyes.

NIGHTFALL

The hour approached, when, stems incline,
the scents in the vesper breezes turn so fine,

A melancholy waltz, repeated daily in drowsiness,
the scraggy shoreline protects bay's blue against sea's
craziness;

How nature senses day's change,
the sunset drowns within this blood-red exchange,

Moon's steely patina appears behind morose clouds,
the tarnished day is now hidden from doubts;

From those archaic stems of those trees, moss drips,
in that lake full of fish and darkness it slips;

Out of that mirror of water, the night's battle cry came,
while clear air objected to night's claim of fame,

While sky's dome, far from clear, showed moons
mournful face
and stars looked on, spread in that sky with grace;

Night's battle won clear day's fight and darkness
prevailed,
taken day's cloak from where it has failed.

SUNSET

I see that roseate evening sky as the sun dies,
sadness rises in me, flooding me with no surprise;
Oh, darkness do I remain alone in this plundered spot,
With poignant memories of that golden light once so
hot;

Gone is the fragile murmuring and that gilded glow,
my mind pillaged by that devouring beast, I don't know;
Gone is that languorous ecstasy of light's feast,
as darkness floods the day's table, that has ceased;

As I tumble down that riverbed in a sleepy complaint,
filled with squalid light and faded paint;
Gone are the fruits, leaf's and branch once green,
now black, as night has glossed it to a sheen;

The nightly fog is still flirting with the breeze,
bringing my hope for early morn to its knees;
The dark forest air now smells bitter,
as I wait for morning's first twitter.

DARK NIGHTS

Sleepy seasons, I do not love or praise,
misty winding-sheets and nebulous days;

As the sun descents in the west,
and the early moon rises like a new flower;

The birds become silent in their nests,
I seek rest and sleep within my stone tower;

The green and happy grove was fully mine,
and now beside that bleating lamb,

Unseen I am waiting for a blessing, divine,
so, I can lie down and sleep, I am,

Time once, I did dream in the tower's shade,
I was forlorn, troubled, and broken,

Now I can walk among those ancient trees that are made,
in that night I am covered with grey despair, unspoken,

In a dangerous world I live hidden under that dark cloud,
and cruelty has set for me her snare,

Spreading the bait with great care,
but I do not fear as I will not be there;

UNABLE

The Moon through the glass is a dreams to-night,
like that fair woman at rest,
under the passing stars, foam of the sky it is;
I dream of beauty that passes like a dream,
mournful that no new wonders may exist,
like the pale waters in their wintry tidal race;

And tall ships with thought-woven sails pass by,
windblown spray coated they follow the tide of hours,
I have sought more than this in rain or morning's dew,
Or on the nightly moon,
or sighs amid my wandering,
or in the air's daily tune

Sound from sea's sad salty lips,
a tightly woven silence, I cannot pass.

AUTUMN'S DREAMS

A fight in the eaves, sparrows perhaps,
while I look at autumn's harvest moon's face,
and the last summer's leaves colour lapse,
all in happy harmony of nature's grace;

A girl arose with those red mournful lips,
the greatness of the world in tears, it seems,
the climbing moon follows those empty ships,
arise, or I will see those clamorous dreams;

The cold wet wind blows from that dark sky,
above the grey river that's there flowing,
in the dark hazel grove the winds will cry,
it's sorrow tales, that's are in't heart show'ng;

> I call, as dreams go by me, one by one,
> doomed, as becalmed ships would have done.

DEWDROPS

Dew forever shining in that soft grey light,
as hope falls, while love will decay in time,
but I go where hills are built in the night,
with sun and the moon and hollows so sublime;

For there is a mystic'l brotherhood there,
and river and stream work out their will,
there, were love is less dear, in that misty air,
dew forever shining with silk'n thread there still;

As the clouds of incense rise in that sky,
so that heavenly eyes can't see or close,
crowns have been hurl'd down for those eyes to cry,
now I am weary of the dream-heavy prose,

Dew forever shining in that grey lady's hair,
and lilies are carried through many a square.

MOONLIGHT

I stand in that moonlit landscape so fair,
in that yellow light, the song rise, firm 'n sweet,
as they celebrate that night's dream, so clear,
the melancholic moon rises to her feet,

Triumphant, roseate and full, as we meet,
birds dream in their basins of smooth white stone.
they walk in the air knowing they must eat,
leaving me quietly to mourn all alone.

Fountains stony and tall full of dying seed,
waiting for that sound full of subtle tone,
as they sob, stony, but firm to their creed,
dreaming of the moonlight, that is now gone.

HIDDEN

One day, a nightly high wind blew them down,
hiding them in the corner of the room,
subtly they would smile, and tried not to frown,
as the marble dust whirl's in that dreamy gloom.

In my dreams, there're days of sadness and doom,
as I pursue those gold and purple butterflies,
o' how sad it's to see that empty tomb,
of those, that know, fly and utter the soft cries;

The branches grow out aspen like a broom,
as courtiers and butterflies bright, still rise,
within that dream, reality will not resume,
as the marble dust whirl's in that dreamy gloom

WHITE WOMAN

White woman with numberless dreams,
the tales woven with soft silken threads

I bring you careful and with reverent hands,
the books of my countless strange loving plans,

White woman passion that was there not before,
tide wears its shallow bed in that sandy shore,

With a heart more older than the horn sound's past,
and those dreams brimmed with pale fire so vast:

White woman of sweet dreams and countless time,
I bring you my heart and passionate rhyme.

MOONLIGHT

Carrying flowers her hands deep in th'se gloves,
the moon's careful dreamy face shows tonight,

Caressing, her hand distraught, but with love,
upon that silken avalanche of light,

I watch the white visions move, past her keep,
which rise like a blossom in the dark sky,

And when, time's wrapped in her languor sleep
her float'ng robe, a royal vision, I can't deny,

Lascivious streams caress her stony face,
concealed from every scornful jest that flies,

Her gloomy beauty; and her sovereign grace,
are made of shade and void; a flower' disguise,

When memory's eyes look back, its remembers,
and recalls the beauty of the caresses,

The charm of evenings by that fire's embers,
the balcony fill'd with veiled rose tresses.

LIVING

When the tears run from my eyes in streams,
I do not regret those past days with you,
my voice will rise, and be heard in your dreams,
and I will resist the tears and sights true;

So long as my sight's clear of visions new,
visions that will praise your female grace,
but my mind can still embrace that old view,
the thought to be one mind to, see your face:

We are like whirling tops and rolling balls,
no longer gives us signs of that love,
even when the dark and sleepy night-time falls,
the cruel angel who goads forth the dove;

       Heed my words, live now and not tomorrow,
       and gather today the roses of life.

FOREST SECRETS

At midnight during the autumn I stand,
beneath the mystic moon she will emerge,
the dewy vapor's soft and unplanned,
exhaled from that golden globe's verge;

The rosemary nods upon the grave,
and lilies floats on waves with icy urge,
a conscious slumber seems to take,
beneath the mystic moon she will emerge;

The hidden airs, as in a wizard rout,
ghosts the shadows rise and fall in moon's light,
flit through your darkened chamber in and out,
beneath the mystic moon she will emerge;

> Far in the forest, trees tall dim and old,
> for them some untold secret's may unfold.

THE SKY IN AUTUMN

In that chilly Autumn's sky, devoid of sound,
countless stars shine cold and round;

With your hand in mine, we saunter,
aimlessly meandering, looking for the star that shines
louder;

These days will not bring Spring,
but we will endure the harsh days that Winter will bring;

Angels will sing when you are near,
together we do not fear.

TWILIGHT SUN

Like the disappearing twilight's sun,
and those glistening impenetrable stars of the night;

Your words touch me like a cool mountain spring,
as an Autumn day, filled with tender rain;

I wait for the emerging flower,
drowned by that rain;

Before Summer's blossoms approach,
flowing out to eternity.

TIDES

Tide rising slowly, engulfing my sanctuary,
fear fills my being,
all is outside, I am protected by my bastion,
stones impregnable by nameless forces;

The tide, my treacherous consort,
reluctant to follow my paths;

Lurking at every corner,
lessening my island of hope;

Swallowing my castle,
engulfed by the never-ending sea.

ANOTHER DREAM

Wind rushes through my life, like a dance of happiness,
cherishing every precious second;

But the bleak winter days are full of fear and wary
dreams,
my bastion 's broken and torn asunder on that fateful
day;

Tide rushes in engulfing and drowning my trusted
fortress,
wind surges through my life invigorating but
distrustful, I would say;

Rebuilding this stony rock,
a task completed within my dreams.

THOUGHTS OF SUMMER

Summer when will I see you again?
alas, my dreams move along paths uncharted;

Trampling those precious blades of summer's grass,
autumn, the austere one, will block my tracks;

Gone are my dreams of briny air scouring my
uncovered head,
will I see you again, my dear Summer;

And feel your bright rays searing my skin,
I am safe inside my dreams;

I Dream of that Summer.